1997

ELVIS PRESLEY

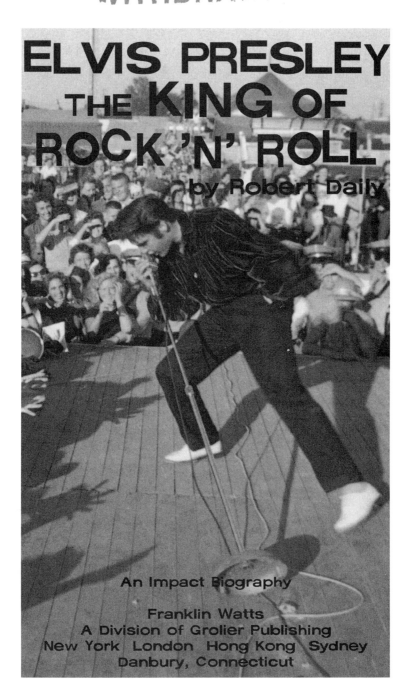

ELVIS PRESLEY
THE KING OF ROCK 'N' ROLL

by Robert Daily

An Impact Biography

Franklin Watts
A Division of Grolier Publishing
New York London Hong Kong Sydney
Danbury, Connecticut

"There have been a lotta tough guys. There have been pretenders. There have been contenders. But there is only one King."
—Bruce Springsteen

To Emma Katherine Daily,
my hunka-hunka-burnin' love

Photo credits ©: AP/Wide World Photos: 15, 73; Archive Photos: 2–3, 62, 55, 59 (both Frank Driggs Collection); Bettmann Archive: 44; Corbis-Bettmann: 48; Graceland: 17, 40; Michael Ochs Archives: 34, 45, 68, 80, 87, 99, 114, 26, 38 (both Colin Escott), 32 (Memphis Brooks Museum); Springer/Bettmann: 66; UPI/Bettmann: 8, 72, 77, 94, 120; UPI/Corbis-Bettmann: 93, 105; Wide World Photos: 129.

Library of Congress Cataloging-in-Publication Data

Daily, Robert.
Elvis Presley : the king of rock 'n' roll / Robert Daily.
p.   cm. — (An Impact biography)
Includes bibliographical references (p.   ) and index.
Summary: Examines the rock star's childhood, family life, musical career, films, and legacy.
ISBN 0-531-11288-8 (lib.bdg.)   ISBN 0-531-15821-7 (pbk.)
1. Presley, Elvis, 1935–1977—Juvenile literature. 2. Rock musicians—United States—Biography—Juvenile literature. [1. Presley, Elvis, 1935–1977.
2. Singers. 3. Rock music.] I. Title.
ML3930.P73D35 1996
782.42166'092—dc20   96-5942
[B]   CIP AC MN

CONTENTS

CHAPTER ONE

THE
ONCE AND FUTURE KING

"As long as [rock 'n' roll] lasts, I'll continue doing it. As long as that's what the people want. And if they change, if it dies out, I'll try to do something else. And if that doesn't work I'll just say, 'Well, I had my day.' "

—Elvis Presley

In Memphis, Tennessee, at 3 A.M., ten thousand people march slowly up a long, curving driveway. Ten thousand points of light flicker in the dark as each worshiper clutches a burning candle. At the top of the hill, the people stop in front of a grave. Some weep uncontrollably. Some pray silently. Some leave behind flowers, love letters, or statues of Jesus Christ.

The grave contains the body of Elvis Presley, the rock 'n' roll singer, who died in 1977. Every year on August 16, the date of his death, his adoring fans travel to Memphis from near and far (as far as Tasmania and China) to celebrate and preserve his memory. For an entire week they eat, sleep, and breathe Elvis Presley. They wear Elvis T-shirts, buy Elvis souvenirs, watch Elvis movies, listen to Elvis music, and swap Elvis stories.

The anniversary of Elvis Presley's death
brings fans from all over the world to the
entertainer's grave site in Memphis,
Tennessee, to pay their respects.

In a Chicago hotel lobby stands a cluster of fifty people identically dressed in sequined jumpsuits, long sideburns, and jet-black hair. A varied group, they are male and female, black and white, ranging in age from fifty-two to seven. They have one thing in common: they make their living impersonating Elvis Presley. When they imitate Elvis on stage, fans scream, scramble for sweat-soaked scarves, toss their room keys (and sometimes their undergarments) on the stage. "An impersonator like myself," explains one performer, "is to Elvis like a priest in a church. They're giving that live performance because God is not there in body."

At a university in Oxford, Mississippi, Elvis's home state, a group of college professors and critics from around the world gathers for a six-day conference called "In Search of Elvis: Music, Race, Religion, Art, Performance." Speakers (many of whom teach college courses about Elvis) compare his song lyrics to William Shakespeare's writings. They discuss his role in bringing pop, rhythm and blues, and country music together. One anthropologist calls Elvis Presley "the greatest popular culture figure of our century."

You are forgiven for wondering, "Why are people so obsessed with Elvis Presley?" After all, he is an entertainer, not a president or an emperor. Furthermore, he is a *dead* entertainer. At the time of the scenes described above, he had been deceased for at least fifteen years.

Yes, Elvis is a phenomenon. He's one of the most curious and interesting phenomena in American music history. Years after his death, people are still listening to, marveling at, and obsessing about Elvis Presley, the King of Rock 'n' Roll.

The facts of his career are impressive. He made it big in movies, television, live performing, and the recording industry. He earned 126 gold and platinum records and placed 114 songs on the Top 40 charts. He sold more than a billion records worldwide (more than any other performer). He starred in thirty-three movies. One of his television appearances drew an unbelievable 82.6 percent of the total television audience. Another attracted an estimated one and a half billion viewers around the globe. In his lifetime, he grossed more than a billion dollars. In death, he has grossed billions more.

In all those numbers, however, there's nothing that explains how Elvis moved so smoothly from famous pop star to international legend, nothing that accounts for the fact that he is worshiped more than any other music idol, dead or alive.

To understand *that*, you have to listen to his music and watch tapes of his performances. Elvis practically invented rock 'n' roll. He brought together a number of influences, and helped bridge the gap between "black" and "white" music. His performing style literally "rocked" the nation; in the quiet of the 1950s, he went off like a stick of dynamite. He forever changed the course of popular music with his voice, his sideburns, and his swiveling hips.

It wasn't just music. Elvis transformed the whole culture, the way that people dressed, talked, acted, thought. In his book *The Fifties*, historian David Halberstam wrote that the three most important events of the 1950s were the *Brown v. Board of Education* Supreme Court decision banning segregated schools, the building of Levittown (an early planned suburban community), and the emergence of Elvis: "In cultural terms, his coming was nothing less than the start of a revolution." The Smithsonian Institution in Washington, D.C., described that emergence as "the single greatest event in the two-hundred-year history of American music." Leonard Bernstein, conductor and composer (of *West Side Story* fame), called him "the greatest cultural force in the 20th century."

Even today, Elvis is a major player in American culture. As a song by rocker Mojo Nixon proclaims, "Elvis Is Everywhere." He is the subject of more than 300 college courses. He is described in more than 160 books and 150 songs. He (that is, an Elvis impersonator) shows up in the Academy Award–winning movie *Forrest Gump*, and in many other films and television programs. Even Bill Clinton once appeared on a television talk show playing "Heartbreak Hotel" on his saxophone.

As the *New York Times* wrote on October 30, 1994, "Try to pass 24 hours in the United States without hearing Elvis Presley's name or seeing his image. It's virtually impossible."

One of the reasons Elvis's story fascinates people is that it's almost a parody of the American dream. His life was storybook stuff, transporting him from rural poverty (he was born in a two-room shack) to international fame. One year he was driving a truck for forty-two dollars a week, and two years later he was making millions and driving a fleet of Cadillacs.

Everything about him—from his fame to, in later years, his waistline—was bigger than life. At every stage of his career, he broke new ground. He exploded on the scene in 1955, created a whole new look and sound, sold millions of records, and shocked a nation. Then he went to Hollywood, starred in thirty-three movies, and almost ruined his career. Then he made a startling comeback, sold millions more records, played Las Vegas, filled giant arenas. Finally he died a tragic and wasteful death, shocked a nation again, and drew more than fifty thousand fans to his funeral.

As a hero, Elvis was definitely flawed. After his death, friends and colleagues revealed that the bright star had a dark side, that, among other things, he'd been addicted to drugs. Even these ugly revelations seemed to fuel the myth. With each new story, the legend grew larger.

Elvis is a complex figure, full of contrasts and contradictions. For this reason he's often misunderstood. Marion Keisker, the woman who played a large part in his discovery, once said of Elvis: "He was like a mirror in a way: whatever you were looking for, you were going to find in him." He's a blank slate, ready to take on whatever meaning people give him. He is rock 'n' roll's savior, or its ruin. The King, or the joker. A saint, or a sinner. Hip, or square. He's a hillbilly cat in pegged pants, he's a rebel in black leather, he's an overweight guy in a rhinestone jumpsuit. All those things or none of them.

Many attempts have been made to understand the Elvis phenomenon. Ultimately, because he provokes such strong opinions, people have to make up their own minds about what Elvis means and why his legend keeps growing. This book presents the facts of Elvis Presley's life. Read them and decide for yourself.

CHAPTER TWO

—— BIRTH ——
OF THE
KING

*"When I was a boy, I was the
hero in comic books and movies.
I grew up believing in a dream."*
—Elvis Presley

Although he would become one of the richest, most
famous human beings on the planet, Elvis Presley was
born into a world of poverty and obscurity. His life is
often described as a fairy tale, but there was nothing
romantic or heroic about his "once upon a time."

His parents, Vernon Elvis Presley and Gladys Love
Smith, were born poor, and knew nothing but tough
times growing up. They both dropped out of school
when they were young. Vernon's father kicked him out of
the house when he was only fifteen. When he married
Gladys, he was working as a sharecropper, a farmer who
works fields for plantation owners in exchange for a share
of the profits.

Gladys also came from a family of poor sharecroppers. Her father died when she was a teenager. She

helped support her family by working behind a sewing machine for thirteen bucks a week. She and Vernon met in the town of Tupelo, Mississippi. They were married in 1933. Vernon, only seventeen, lied and said he was twenty-two, while the older Gladys knocked two years off her age and claimed to be nineteen.

In 1934 Vernon built a house in East Tupelo, a separate town on the wrong side of the tracks, where sharecroppers and poor factory workers lived. Today this house—Elvis's birthplace—is open to the public. It has been spruced up for tourists: painted, wallpapered, landscaped, and electrified. But make no mistake, when the Presleys lived there it was no showplace. Known as a shotgun shack because you could shoot a bullet through the front door and out the back without hitting anything, the two-room building had dirt floors. Although Tupelo had recently been electrified, there was no electricity, or running water. The Presleys relied on oil lamps and an outhouse. Gladys kept chickens and a cow in a dirt backyard.

At 4 A.M. on January 8, 1935, Gladys gave birth to twins. The first, named Jesse Garon, was stillborn. Thirty-five minutes later the second baby appeared, perfectly healthy. He was named Elvis Aron Presley. Elvis was his father's middle name; Aron came from the Bible. (It's traditionally spelled "Aaron" but Vernon, with only an eighth-grade education, misspelled it on the birth certificate.)

Jesse Presley was buried in an unmarked grave in a Tupelo cemetery. He was never forgotten. Gladys often told Elvis that "when one twin died, the one that lived got all the strength of both." As a boy, Elvis frequently visited his brother's grave. Years later, as an adult, he talked about him often; there were rumors that he even talked *to* Jesse, looking for that strength.

In 1937, when Elvis was two, his father was arrested for forging a four-dollar check. Although the amount was small, Vernon was sentenced to three years at Parchman

Elvis Presley was born in this two-room home in Tupelo, Mississippi, in 1935.

Penitentiary, a work camp. He ended up serving only eight months, but his prison stint was a source of shame to the family for the rest of their lives.

When Vernon went to prison, the Presleys lost their house. During the next decade they lived in one rented shack or another, often moving just before the rent was due. For a time they lived across the street from Shake Rag, Tupelo's lively black neighborhood. Vernon worked a string of odd jobs: carpenter, milkman, deliveryman, and general laborer. Gladys picked cotton, carrying baby Elvis around the fields in a cotton sack. The family often went hungry. At times they lived on nothing but corn bread and water.

All these hardships brought the Presleys closer together. Gladys, who had already lost one baby and was unable to have another, showered all her love and attention on Elvis. They were unusually close. She communicated with him in baby talk, and he called her pet names (Sat'nin' was a favorite). Until he was a teenager she walked him to school every day, hand in hand at first. Then she walked on the other side of the street so as not to embarrass him. Once, when an older bully picked on Elvis, Gladys defended her son with a broom. "My mama never let me out of her sight," Elvis recalled in later years. "I couldn't go down to the creek with the other kids."

Said a Tupelo neighbor of the Presleys, "Gladys thought he was the greatest thing that ever happened and treated him that way. She worshiped that child from the day he was borned to the day she died."

＊＊＊＊

What kind of boy was Elvis Presley? By all accounts he was quiet, shy, polite, the kind of kid you might never pick out of a crowd. He was only "an average student," according to one of his teachers. He had few friends. A gentle boy, he hated the idea of hunting. His favorite pastime was reading comic books, especially Captain Marvel, and dreaming about the future. He had an active fantasy life, imagining himself to be successful, famous, and rich—a movie star, maybe. To his mother he once said: "Don't you worry none, baby. When I grow up, I'm going to buy you a fine house and pay everything you owe at the grocery store and get two Cadillacs—one for you and Daddy, and one for me."

Although his parents were not musicians, young Elvis was always attracted to music. He and Gladys were radio junkies, addicted to country programs, especially a show called the "Grand Ole Opry," broadcast live every Saturday night. He also listened to hillbilly music on Tupelo

Gladys and Vernon Presley with young Elvis

station WELO. "He was crazy about music," said one of his classmates. "That's all he talked about."

Music was also an important element at the Tupelo First Assembly of God Church, which the Presleys attended every Sunday. Services at this Pentecostal church were very emotional, with pastors speaking in tongues and healing the sick. The church appealed to poor members because it preached a hopeful message: the last shall be first.

With its flamboyant musical performances, the church attracted music lovers like Elvis. Even as a youngster he threw himself into singing gospel. Gladys remembered this scene: "When Elvis was just a little fellow, not more than two years old, he would slide down off my lap, run into the aisle, and scramble up to the platform. There he would stand looking at the choir and trying to sing with them. He was too little to know the words . . . but he could carry the tune and he would watch their faces and try to do as they did."

When he was ten he made his solo debut, entering a talent contest at the annual Mississippi-Alabama Fair and Dairy Show in downtown Tupelo. Standing before an audience of hundreds, he sang a country tune called "Old Shep," a sad, sentimental song about a boy and his dog. He finished fifth. According to legend he won five dollars and free admission to all the rides. Probably more exciting to Elvis, his performance was broadcast live over station WELO.

Not long after the contest, Elvis got his first guitar at the Tupelo Hardware Company. The occasion was his eleventh birthday. According to one version of the story, he really wanted a bicycle but the family couldn't afford it. According to F. L. Bobo, operator of Tupelo Hardware, Elvis actually wanted a rifle. "He told his mother he didn't have enough money to buy the guitar and so she said, 'I'll pay up for you, but I can't pay up if it's to buy a rifle,' " Bobo recalled. Though Vernon Presley once said he "never saw a guitar player was worth a damn," he laid out the money for the instrument.

Years later, Elvis said of his father's twelve-dollar purchase: "It was the best investment he ever made."

Elvis learned to play the guitar from a variety of sources—his uncle Vester, his pastor, a WELO disc jockey named Mississippi Slim, and a book of chords. He played for church services, and occasionally performed on a WELO amateur hour, along with many local kids. In the seventh grade he started bringing the guitar to school every day. (In the eighth grade some of the rough kids at school cut the strings on his guitar, but other classmates took up a collection to buy him another set.) "He loved that guitar," his cousin Hershell Presley recalled. "It didn't have but three strings on it most of the time, but he sure could beat the dickens outta it."

During lunch hour, Elvis and a friend would go down to the basement to play and sing country or gospel tunes in front of a few classmates. Someday, he told them, he'd be singing on the "Grand Ole Opry."

In 1948 the Presleys sold their furniture, loaded their clothes into a 1937 Plymouth, and drove north along Route 78 to the city of Memphis, Tennessee. Elvis was thirteen.

In the South of the 1940s and 1950s, moving to the big city, where steady work was more plentiful, was a common way to escape poverty. (In 1900, 15 percent of all Southerners lived in cities; by 1960 the number had risen to 55 percent.) Gladys got a job as a sewing-machine operator. Vernon packed boxes for eighty-five cents an hour. For a few months the family lived in the slums of Memphis, moving from one single room to another, usually sharing a bathroom with several other families. In 1949 they were accepted into a federal housing project known as Lauderdale Courts. Their two-bedroom apartment, with its own bathroom and a nice grass yard, was a step up from the single rooms they had known.

Elvis enrolled at L. C. Humes High School, which went from seventh to twelfth grade. Moving from Tupelo was not an easy adjustment for him. On his first day at the school of sixteen hundred students, he came home early, looking "so nervous he was bug-eyed," Vernon recalled. "He said he didn't know where the office was and classes had started and there were so many kids. He was afraid they'd laugh at him."

Big-city Elvis was not much different from small-town Elvis. He was shy. (At his senior prom he never danced once, saying he didn't know how.) He wasn't especially popular, though he made friends with a few of the guys at the Lauderdale Courts. They'd play football, go to movies, or wander around downtown Memphis.

Elvis also worked odd jobs. He ushered at the movies, mowed lawns, and even sold his blood for money. His senior year he worked a 3 P.M. to 11:30 P.M. shift at a furniture factory. He later quit because he couldn't stay awake during class.

At Humes High, he majored in industrial arts. He earned only a C in music. When his teacher told him he couldn't sing, he told her she just didn't appreciate *his* kind of music. The next day he brought his guitar to class and sang a popular tune called "Keep Them Cold Icy Fingers Off of Me." When he finished, the teacher agreed: she *didn't* like his kind of music.

Still, he persevered; he kept playing and learning. Living in Memphis in the 1950s and listening to the city's many radio stations was a great education for an aspiring musician like Elvis. Memphis was a magnet for performers of all kinds of music, especially country, gospel, and rhythm and blues.

Country music he already knew. But Memphis broadened his knowledge. He used to hang out at radio station WMPS, watching Bob Neal's live broadcast of "High Noon Roundup," a country program. In 1953 he hitch-hiked 240 miles (386 km) to Meridian, Mississippi, to sing in a talent contest at the Jimmie Rodgers "Father of Country Music" festival.

In the 1950s, Memphis was a headquarters for white

gospel musicians. Elvis was a regular audience member at the All-Night Gospel Sings at Ellis Auditorium, where the top white gospel groups of the day sang into the wee hours of the morning. He loved the harmonies and the emotional performance style of quartets like the Blackwood Brothers and the Statesmen. The flamboyant movements and flashy clothes of Statesmen lead singer Jake Hess made a big impression on Elvis.

He also loved black gospel. He and his girlfriend would sneak out of their First Assembly of God Church and drive to a nearby black church, where he was captivated by the music. Sometimes they'd return to that church at night for the live broadcast of WHBQ's "Camp Meeting of the Air," a program that combined preaching and black gospel.

The third style that captured Elvis's attention during the early 1950s was rhythm and blues, or R&B. On Memphis radio station WDIA, "The Mother Station of the Negroes," he listened to the best of the R&B musicians—Sonny Boy Williamson and Howlin' Wolf (both from Memphis) and Ruth Brown and Little Junior Parker. Across town, at station WHBQ, a disc jockey named Dewey Phillips played R&B and Negro spirituals on a nightly radio show called "Red Hot and Blue." Elvis bought the latest R&B records, as well as some classic oldies, at a store called Charlie's Record Shop. If he couldn't afford to buy, he and his girlfriend would just sit in the shop, drinking Cokes and listening to song after song.

Elvis also learned R&B straight from the source—the famous Beale Street, located half a mile (0.8 km) from the Presley home. A seedy stretch of clubs and shops, Beale was a mecca for well-known Memphis R&B musicians. Blues legend B. B. King remembers running into a young Elvis at a pawn shop where R&B greats used to gather.

Soon after he discovered Beale Street, Elvis started to remake his image. He began shopping at Lansky Brothers, at the end of Beale, where R&B greats Little Milton and Rufus Thomas bought their sharp duds. He liked to wear dress pants (never jeans, like the other kids), brightly colored shirts (pink was his favorite), a sport jacket, and maybe a scarf around his neck like a movie star. His Humes High classmates thought he was "weird," according to one friend. "Of course he got a lot of flak. . . . He stood out like a sore thumb."

His wild clothes were nothing, though, compared to his hair. Elvis was obsessed with his hair. He wore it longer than the other kids, and used three different oils, including Rose Oil tonic and Vaseline, to slick it back. He also let his sideburns grow long. He was constantly fussing with his hair, combing it, shaping it, stroking it. It was a way of calling attention to himself. At school, his hair caused him no end of grief. He was kicked off the football team when he refused to cut it. On another occasion, his friend Red West recalled, "all the guys were gonna get him and cut his hair. I helped him escape from that."

* * * *

After leaving Humes in 1953 (the first in his family to graduate from high school), Elvis went to work for Crown Electric Company, an electrical contracting firm. He drove a truck, earning about forty-two dollars a week. But he knew his future was not in trucking. He always carried his guitar in the back of the Crown truck; whenever he wasn't working, he was playing and singing. Music was becoming more and more important in his life. He loved the attention it brought him. In his senior year at Humes he had performed at the annual talent show, and "it was amazing how popular I became after that," he said.

At night, young Elvis Presley would sit on the steps outside his Lauderdale Courts apartment, singing softly and strumming his guitar in the dark. And dreaming of glory.

CHAPTER THREE

——— 706 ———
UNION AVENUE

*"He tried not to show it, but he
felt so inferior. Elvis Presley
probably innately was the most
introverted person that [ever]
came into that studio. He
didn't play with bands. . . . All
he did was sit with his guitar
on the side of his bed at home."*
—Sam Phillips

At the corner of Main and Union in Memphis, 706
Union Avenue to be exact, there stands a squat brick
building, red with white trim, with a red-and-blue neon
sign in the plate-glass window that reads Memphis
Recording Service. It's the sort of anonymous-looking
building you might easily pass right by. And yet rock fans
(including famous musicians like the band members of
U2, Ringo Starr, Tom Petty, and Bonnie Raitt) travel
from around the world to pass through this tiny space. In
their eyes, this building—the home of Sun Records—is a
shrine, a mythical place where a nineteen-year-old truck
driver was transformed into a superstar in the space of
just two years.

In the four-plus decades since Elvis Presley was "discovered" at Sun Studios, the story has become wrapped

in legend and myth; some of the facts have been obscured. One thing, though, seems certain—Elvis would never have been crowned the King of Rock 'n' Roll without Sun Records and a man named Sam Phillips.

* * * *

It was a sweltering, sticky summer afternoon in 1953 when Elvis Presley showed up at the door of the Memphis Recording Service, whose motto declared, "We record anything—anywhere—anytime." Seated in the reception area were several customers waiting to make their very own double-sided acetate records for $3.98 (plus tax).

According to legend, Elvis was there to record two songs as a birthday present for Gladys Presley. However, since his mother's birthday had already passed, and since he could have recorded his voice at a five-and-dime down the street for only a quarter, it's more likely that he was trying to catch the eyes and ears of Sam Phillips, owner of the Memphis Recording Service and founder of Sun Records.

Born in 1923, Sam Phillips is one of the most important figures in rock 'n' roll history. He started working as a disc jockey at the age of eighteen but grew tired of the big band sound that was popular at the time. What Phillips liked was music that was different. Music that was fresh, rough, and raw. Music that came straight from the gut.

What he liked was rhythm and blues, the music of black Americans. His goal at Sun was "to make records with some of those great Negro artists," he explained. "It just seemed to me that [these artists] were the only ones who had any frankness left in their music." He especially liked working with amateurs because their music had a natural, unpracticed feeling—a nice contrast to the polished pop music that was popular in the 1950s.

Phillips started Sun Records in 1950. When he did,

local R&B artists stopped traveling to Chicago to make their records and started heading over to 706 Union Avenue. By 1953 he was the most important independent music producer in Memphis. When he wasn't making records with blues greats like Junior Parker, Howlin' Wolf, and B. B. King, he was looking for the next big performer. Although Phillips later denied saying it, Marion Keisker, his secretary and assistant, remembered hearing him proclaim, "If I could find a white man who had the Negro sound and the Negro feel, I could make a million dollars."

The day Elvis entered the Memphis Recording Service, however, Sam Phillips was not there; he was out eating lunch. Marion Keisker was running the studio by herself. She took note of Presley's long, greasy hair, sideburns, and unusual clothes, and wondered (she later recalled) "if he wanted a handout." When he said he wanted to make a record, she asked, "Who do you sound like?"

"I don't sound like nobody," he answered politely as he paced about the small room, waiting for his turn at the microphone.

Imagine the young man's excitement as he was ushered back to the 18-by-30-foot (5.5-by-9-m) studio, where his R&B heroes had cut his favorite records. Imagine his nervousness, too, as Marion Keisker turned on the recording equipment and told him to start singing.

The session happened quickly. Strumming his beat-up guitar, Elvis sang two songs, "My Happiness" and "That's When Your Heartaches Begin," ballads made popular by an R&B group called the Ink Spots. "My Happiness" was a tune he had sung over and over for friends at the Lauderdale Courts.

Although his voice was raw and his guitar-picking strictly amateur, Marion Keisker decided the boy showed some promise. In the middle of "My Happiness" she

Music producer Sam Phillips in his Memphis
recording studio

turned on a second recorder, making a copy for Phillips to hear. Later she took down the boy's name (misspelling it "Elvis Pressley"). Because the Presleys didn't have a telephone, Elvis gave her the number of his next-door neighbor. After this number Marion Keisker wrote: "Good ballad singer. Hold."

* * * *

Elvis returned to Sun Records about six months later, on January 4, 1954, a few days shy of his nineteenth birthday. This time Sam Phillips himself was there. He ran the equipment while Elvis recorded—again at his own expense—another two ballads, "Casual Love Affair" and "I'll Never Stand in Your Way." Phillips agreed with Keisker that Presley was a talented ballad singer. He told the young man that if he came across a song suited to his style, he would call him.

During the next few months, Presley would find any excuse to drop by Sun Records—to say hello or to ask Keisker if she knew of any bands looking for a singer. (In 1954 he auditioned for a local group. When they turned him down, telling him "You're never going to make it as a singer," he was bitterly disappointed.) It wasn't until June that Sam Phillips found a reason to call Elvis. He came across a song, called "Without You," which he thought could be a hit with the right singer. Keisker remembered the young man who kept stopping by.

"What about the kid with the sideburns?" she asked. Phillips agreed.

"I called and asked him at his convenience to come see us," Keisker remembered. "I turned around, and there was Elvis coming through the door. I think he ran all the way." Later in his career Elvis would joke, "I was an overnight sensation. A year after they heard me the first time, they called me back!"

In the studio, Phillips guided him through several

takes of "Without You." After a few hours it became clear that this was not a song that would bring out the best in Elvis. So Phillips asked him to sing anything else he knew. Elvis sang *everything* else he knew. "It seemed like he had a photographic memory for every damn song he ever heard," Phillips recalled. Elvis sang snippets from a number of tunes, including several ballads recorded by a pop singer named Dean Martin—certainly nothing that would be considered rock 'n' roll. ("I had never sung anything but slow music and ballads in my life at that time," he would say later.) Phillips turned off the recorder and just listened.

Although nothing came of that first session, Phillips kept "the kid with the sideburns" in the back of his mind. A few days later, he was talking to a Memphis guitar player named Scotty Moore. Moore was looking for a singer. Phillips suggested he call Elvis. "The best I remember," said Phillips, "he can sing pretty good."

On July 4, Elvis showed up at Moore's house for an audition, wearing his trademark hepcat outfit: pink shirt, black pants, and white shoes. Joining them was Bill Black, a bass player and friend of Moore. They sat in Moore's living room and tried to find some musical common ground, playing whatever song popped into their heads. The older men were not impressed. "He was green as a gourd," recalled Moore. Black felt he was "nothing out of the ordinary." After Elvis left, Moore called Phillips and said, "He didn't really knock me out." Still, Phillips asked the two musicians to bring Elvis into the studio so he could hear how they all sounded together.

The next night, the trio met at Sun Records around seven. They kept struggling to find songs they all knew, trying a few slow-moving ballads like "I Love You Because" and "Harbor Lights." Nothing clicked.

After a few hours they were ready to quit. The guys were sitting around drinking Cokes and coffee when—as

Elvis remembered it later—"this song popped into my head that I had heard years ago, and I started kidding around with [it]." The song was "That's All Right (Mama)," a rhythm and blues number recorded by Arthur "Big Boy" Crudup in 1946. Elvis stood up and sang, "jumping around and acting the fool," in Moore's words. Moore and Black joined in. The lyrics were simple, almost nonsensical:

Well that's all right mama
That's all right for you
That's all right mama
Just any way you do . . .

Phillips came running back into the studio. "What was that?" he asked. "What are you doing?"

"We don't know," said the three men.

"Well, back up," said Phillips, "try to find a place to start, and do it again."

They played the song nine times before recording a version they all liked. "That's All Right" was just what Sam Phillips was looking for—a simple song, sung from the gut. It was "raw and ragged," said Scotty Moore. "We thought it was exciting, but what was it? It was just so completely different."

* * * *

Yes—what *was* it? Nobody knew what to name this music, simply because it hadn't existed before. Eventually, though, people would label this new sound *rock 'n' roll.*

Years later, there would be controversy over whether Elvis Presley "invented" rock 'n' roll. In a sense, this argument is pointless. Rock 'n' roll was not invented by any one individual; it evolved over a number of years. While Elvis was still in school, black singers like Wynonie Harris and Fats Domino were planting the roots of rock.

In 1951 a gentleman named Jackie Brenston came to Sam Phillips and recorded a song called "Rocket 88," considered by many to be the first rock 'n' roll record. Elvis was •not even the first *white* musician to sing rock 'n' roll. Bill Haley and the Comets had already reached the charts with "Crazy, Man, Crazy." In 1951 Haley also recorded "Rocket 88" (after Brenston had made his recording), and his version is considered by some to be the first rock 'n' roll record by a white artist.

So what Elvis did was not unprecedented. But it was original; it was unique. In "That's All Right," and the dozen more records he would make for Sun Records, he took the many musical forms that had influenced him—country, gospel, R&B, pop—and integrated them into a distinct new sound. Elvis's sound was bluesier than country, twangier than R&B. It offered the sexuality of blues music, the smoothness of pop, and the exuberance of gospel. Above all, it had his charisma, the indescribable spark he brought to that tiny room at 706 Union Avenue.

In later years, Elvis was accused of stealing from R&B singers, of slapping a white face on a sound that was invented by blacks. This was unfair. He wasn't just copying the black artists of the 1950s; he was giving their sound a new spin. Also, he never denied his debt to R&B. In 1956 he said, "The colored folks have been singing it and playing it just the way I'm doing now, man, for more years than I know. They played it like that in the shanties and in their juke joints, and nobody paid it no mind till I goosed it up." (Carl Perkins, another Sun rocker, put it this way: "All we did was take country music and give it a colored beat.") Whether he meant to or not, Elvis made it possible for black singers and songwriters to reach larger audiences. His music helped break racial and cultural barriers.

So Elvis Presley and Sam Phillips didn't invent rock 'n' roll all by themselves. But they did—in the space of one minute and fifty-six seconds—change the face of popular music forever.

* ⁎ * ⁎

Disc jockey Dewey Phillips (no relation to Sam) was a very popular guy in Memphis and a friend of Sam's. As host of WHBQ's "Red Hot and Blue," he made a name for himself playing "boogies, blues, and spirituals," according to a *Memphis Commercial Appeal* article. In other words, he played black music for an audience that was both black and white. If Dewey promoted a song, it was almost certain to become a hit. According to critic Peter Guralnick, Dewey's "role in the popularization of rock 'n' roll and rhythm and blues cannot be overstated."

On July 7, Sam Phillips played "That's All Right (Mama)" for his friend. Dewey Phillips didn't know what to make of the record, saying, "It's not black, it's not white, it's not pop, it's not country." He played it over and over. Finally, he decided to introduce the song on his radio show the next night.

"That's All Right" was first heard by Memphis radio listeners at around 9:30 P.M. on the night of July 8, 1954. The response was immediate and overwhelming. The audience flipped. Legend has it that Dewey Phillips received forty-seven phone calls and fourteen telegrams in praise of the song and that he played it either seven, eleven, or thirteen times in a row.

Where was Elvis during all this hubbub? At the movies. He was afraid to listen to Dewey's show because "I thought people would laugh at me," he later told a journalist. So he turned the radio to WHBQ, gave his parents strict instructions to listen, and went to see a western double feature. When Dewey Phillips called the Presley home that evening, he spoke to Gladys. "Mrs. Presley," he said, "you just get that cotton-picking son of yours down here to the station. I played that record

America's first rock 'n' roll star in 1954

of his, and them birdbrain phones haven't stopped ringing since."

Gladys and Vernon found Elvis at the theater and dragged him over to the WHBQ studios. "I was scared to death," Elvis recalled. "I was shaking all over, I just couldn't believe it, but Dewey kept telling me to cool it, [this] was really happening."

Dewey told Elvis he was going to interview him on the air in a few minutes. While they chatted, however, Dewey—sensing the boy's nervousness—secretly turned on the microphone. Dewey asked him where he lived, where he worked, where he went to school. When Elvis said he had graduated from Humes, listeners knew that this singer with a black sound was actually white, since Humes was an all-white school. At the end of their conversation, Dewey thanked Elvis for stopping by the station. "Aren't you going to interview me?" Elvis asked.

"I already have," said Dewey. "The mike's been open the whole time." And so Elvis Presley, age nineteen, was introduced to the world.

After the speedy success of "That's All Right," Sam Phillips needed another song to put on the record's flip side. Elvis, Scotty, and Bill recorded "Blue Moon of Kentucky," an old country song, except that country fans barely recognized it after Elvis speeded up the pace and gave it an odd kind of syncopated beat. In this one little 45-rpm record, you can see the influences that shaped rock 'n' roll music. On one side is a blues number, a black song sung by a white boy raised on gospel. On the other is a traditional hillbilly tune, performed with exuberant energy and a rocking beat.

By the time the record was released, on July 19, 1954, six thousand people had already ordered copies. Elvis and a friend went to the factory in Memphis to watch the first 45-rpm records come off the press. According to the friend, Elvis was "like a little kid at Christmas." He later

Elvis Presley's first record, "That's All Right," was an original combination of musical genres that included country, gospel, blues, and pop.

took a copy of the record to the Rainbow skating rink, one of his old hangouts, and played it over and over again on the jukebox. As far as Elvis was concerned, it didn't get any better than this.

* * * *

On July 30, Elvis made his first appearance in front of a big audience. The place was the outdoor Overton Park band shell in Memphis. The concert's headliner was a country musician named Slim Whitman. Elvis was billed in a newspaper advertisement as "Ellis Presley."

When he took the stage, his knees were knocking so loud you could almost hear them, said Scotty Moore. "I was scared stiff," Elvis later recalled.

Well, not exactly *stiff*. Onstage, Elvis's nervous energy passed through his body and ended up in his legs. He started wiggling and jiggling; his whole body twitched. When Scotty and Bill played an instrumental solo, Elvis stepped back from the microphone and shook even more.

The crowd went wild. After exhausting his repertoire of two songs, Elvis ran offstage and asked Moore what everybody was hollering at. "It was your leg, man!" Moore laughed. "It was the way you were shakin' your left leg!"

This is how Elvis remembered the concert later:

> *Everybody was hollering, and I didn't know what they were hollering at. . . . I came offstage and my manager told me that they was hollering because I was wiggling. And so I went back out for an encore, and I did a little more. And the more I did, the wilder they went.*

It was the first time Elvis Presley provoked a crazed response from a crowd. It certainly would not be the last.

CHAPTER FOUR

—— GOOD ——
ROCKIN' TONIGHT

*"Ain't nowhere else in the world
where you can go from driving
a truck to driving a Cadillac
overnight."*

—Elvis Presley

In September 1954, Elvis recorded his second Sun single, "Good Rockin' Tonight," with "I Don't Care If the Sun Don't Shine" on the flip side. The song, a hard-rocking R&B classic, had been recorded twice before, in 1947 and 1948, both times by black artists. Elvis's version moved quickly up the charts. Meanwhile, his "Blue Moon of Kentucky" reached the top of the Memphis country charts and sold more than twenty thousand copies nationally.

The success of the first two records helped him get concert bookings. He started small, playing local clubs or singing from the back of a flatbed truck at the opening of a local drugstore (for a fee of ten dollars). But in October, Sam Phillips got him booked on one of the biggest radio programs in the country—the "Grand Ole Opry."

Having grown up listening to the "Opry," Elvis must have been overwhelmed to appear on the show, especially as a teenager. Unfortunately, his performance was not exactly a smash. "Opry" audiences were used to more traditional country singers. They didn't know what to make of this wailing, wiggling boy with his drums and electric guitars. When he played his jazzed-up "Blue Moon of Kentucky," they responded with mild applause. Afterward, the show's talent coordinator suggested that Elvis go back to driving a truck.

Despite the lukewarm reception, he was asked to perform on a similar radio show called the "Louisiana Hayride." The "Hayride" audiences were more open to new acts; country stars like Hank Williams and Slim Whitman had debuted on the show. After getting past his initial nervousness, Elvis put on a good show, and the audience exploded. The "Hayride" signed him on as a Saturday-night regular. The contract, which lasted one year, called for Elvis to receive eighteen dollars per show.

With their success on the charts and on the radio, Elvis, Scotty, and Bill—now known as the Blue Moon Boys—were ready to hit the road. Dewey Phillips bought Elvis a used Lincoln sedan for $450. In November Elvis quit his job at Crown Electric. His daddy always said he never knew a guitar player worth a damn, but it looked like Elvis might amount to something after all.

"Music should be something that makes you gotta move, inside or outside."
—Elvis Presley

At the end of 1954, Elvis asked local disc jockey Bob Neal to handle his performance dates. Neal—who had hired Elvis for his first concert (at Overton Park)—started

A nineteen-year-old Elvis joins Scotty Moore (left) and Bill Black on a weekly broadcast of "Louisiana Hayride," one of their first professional gigs.

booking the band at civic clubs, schools, and roadhouses across the South and the Southwest.

For the next year they were always on the go, with shows almost every night. They bounced between big cities like Houston and Dallas, and tiny towns like Hawkins, Texas, and Corinth, Mississippi. "We'd do a show and get offstage and get in the car and drive to the next town and sometimes just get there in time to wash up [and] do the show," Elvis later recalled. He slept—when he slept—in the car. By March, he had saved enough money to realize a lifelong dream: he bought himself a pink Cadillac.

Though he wasn't used to being away from home, Elvis quickly took to life on the road. Mischievous and fun-loving, he was a fan of firecrackers and joy buzzers. "He loved pranks and practical jokes," recalled Scotty Moore. "He was a typical teenager."

As Elvis gained more experience, he grew bolder and more confident onstage. And as he grew bolder, he started creating a sensation wherever he played.

Girls, in particular, responded to his act with total abandon. They stood on their chairs. They danced in the aisles. They screamed, hollered, and wailed. (One rumor said that Bob Neal was paying them fifty cents each to scream.) Elvis was no fool; he learned to play to the audience, teasing them with every wiggle. The girls couldn't help themselves, and neither could he. Said a musician who toured with him in 1955, "He just *had* it."

Nobody quite knew what to make of this young rebel. First, there was his appearance. His clothes were outrageous: two-tone shoes and suits of pink, kelly green, or chartreuse. He spent hours on his hair, which swooped up high on top and cascaded down to a greasy ducktail in the back. Adults who met him remembered "rings of dirt" on his neck.

Elvis bought his first Cadillac in 1955.

Offstage, Elvis was shy, quiet, and polite. He could "yes sir" or "yes ma'am" an adult to death. Onstage, he was transformed. He bounded onto the stage as though he'd been shot out of a cannon. Clutching the mike in a death grip, he bounced on the balls of his feet, his legs twitching and wiggling every which way (a motion that "was half nervousness, half moving to the beat," he later admitted). One observer said it was "like an earthquake in progress."

Bob Luman, a young country singer who saw Elvis perform in 1955, gave this eyewitness account:

> *This cat came out in red pants and a green coat and a pink shirt and socks, and he had this sneer on his face, and he stood behind the mike for five minutes, I'll bet, before he made a move. Then he hit his guitar a lick, and he broke two strings. So there he was, these two strings dangling, and he hadn't done anything yet, and these high school girls were screaming and fainting and running up on the stage, and then he started to move his hips real slow like he had a thing for his guitar.*

It was shocking. It was wild. It was an act of rebellion. Elvis was completely uninhibited onstage. He would snarl, belch into the mike, spit his chewing gum into the audience. He pounded his guitar so fiercely that he broke a string nearly every time he played.

"Sometimes I think my heart is going to explode," he said of his onstage gyrations. Although he didn't know exactly what he had or what he was doing, he *had* it . . . and he *did* it. And he kept doing it, town after town, night after night, despite the growing hysteria that greeted every performance.

Said Elvis: "If I stand still while I'm singing, I'm dead, man. I might as well go back to driving a truck."

* * * *

When he wasn't whipping up a frenzy on the road, Elvis found time, a few days here or a week there, to venture into the studio with Sam Phillips and record new songs for release under the Sun label. Together they continued breaking new ground in rock 'n' roll music.

Presley's 1954 Sun recording of "Milkcow Blues Boogie" illustrates the changes he was making in contemporary music. The tune was an old country favorite—a silly song about a man pining for his sweetheart—and Elvis begins singing it slowly, respectfully. But after a few bars he cuts in. "Hold it, fellas," he snarls. "That don't *move*. Let's get real, real *gone* for a change." Suddenly the tempo doubles. Electric instruments kick in. His voice takes on a harder edge. In the space of this single song, you can hear Elvis turning country music into rock.

Or . . . into *something*. Nobody knew what to call this music. People were forced to invent new words and terms to describe his radical new sound. Some called it "race" music, some called it "pop," some called it "folk." Some labeled it "bopping hillbilly" or "bebop." Later, people dubbed it "rockabilly," a combination of rock and hillbilly. One Memphis newspaper writer heard "a curious blending" of R&B (or "Negro field jazz") and country. Another paper described it as "a white man's voice singing Negro rhythms with a rural flavor."

"It was like a giant wedding ceremony," said Marion Keisker. "It was like two feuding clans [country and R&B] who had been brought together by marriage."

In truth, Elvis had no one style. He was, as critic Peter Guralnick writes, "a man with too many rough edges for anyone ever to smooth away." Every time he visited the Sun studios in 1955, he broke new ground. Songs like "Baby, Let's Play House" and "I'm Left, You're Right, She's Gone" practically exploded with energy.

* * * *

The way Elvis lit up a crowd, it was bound to happen: a full-fledged riot. On May 13, 1955, at the end of a concert in Jacksonville, Florida, he made an innocent, almost teasing suggestion to fourteen thousand wailing fans: "Thank you, girls, I'll see you all backstage."

42

It was all he needed to say. The audience erupted. They went from enthusiastic to insane in a matter of seconds. Screaming fans followed him backstage, poured through an open window into the locker room, ripped his boots off, and tore his clothes to shreds. Elvis escaped on top of a shower. Outside, girls used safety pins to scratch their names and telephone numbers into his Cadillac; others smeared theirs on with lipstick.

Soon every concert turned into a free-for-all. Insanity became the norm. At a Mississippi high school he was attacked onstage by a horde of girls and had to be rescued by his mother and father. In Alabama, hundreds of girls chased him across a football field. At a second concert in Jacksonville, the local paper reported that concertgoers "relieved him of his tie, handkerchiefs, belt, and the greater part of his coat and shirt." Policemen and firemen were enlisted to protect the young singer from his adoring fans.

In 1955, Elvis ventured out of the South for the first time, playing a concert in Cleveland, Ohio. The result was the same: pure pandemonium, proving that his success was not just a southern phenomenon.

Elvis had to be a little frightened by the hysteria he was creating. Publicly, however, he played it cool. "I don't mind if the fans rip the shirt from my back," he said. "They put it there in the first place."

*****

The riots did not escape the attention of a man named Thomas Parker. Known as Colonel Tom, or simply the Colonel (although he never served in the Army), Parker was born in 1910 to parents who worked for circuses and carnivals. After being orphaned, he traveled with the circus; at seventeen he had his own monkey-and-pony act. He later became a dogcatcher and then a press agent and a manager, guiding country singers Eddy Arnold and Hank Snow to stardom.

Elvis surrounded by enthusiastic
fans—mostly teenaged girls

Crude, uneducated, overweight, the Colonel was a
colorful figure with a mysterious past. Rumors swirled
about his carnival days—that he had once painted spar-
rows yellow and sold them as parakeets, or made chickens
"dance" by placing them on a hot plate covered with
straw. Fact or fiction, these stories contained a germ of
truth. Parker was a shrewd hustler, a tough businessman,

In 1955, Colonel Tom Parker became Elvis Presley's manager, a position he held for the rest of the singer's career.

and a ruthless competitor. Said a former associate, "I don't think anyone has beaten him on a deal. . . . He laid the law down, and you went that way or you didn't play."

In 1955, Parker followed Elvis's rise with great interest. He saw in this young man tremendous potential for profit on a national scale. He took special notice when, in July, "Baby, Let's Play House" rose to number ten on the national country charts. It was Elvis's first top-ten single. In the summer of 1955, the Colonel offered the Presleys his services, suggesting that he replace Bob Neal as Elvis's manager.

In August, Vernon and Gladys Presley signed a contract making Colonel Tom Parker Elvis's "special adviser." (Still a minor, Elvis could not sign the contract himself.) By November, the Colonel had engineered a deal for Sam Phillips to sell Presley's contract to RCA Records, a major national recording company. The deal gave RCA the rights to all the Sun songs plus any future recordings. RCA paid Phillips $35,000 plus $5,000 in royalties—an unheard-of fee for an unknown talent. It also gave Elvis a $5,000 advance so he could buy a new Cadillac.

Why would Sam Phillips sell the rights to his most promising singer? He needed the money; he had gone nearly bankrupt getting his business off the ground. Phillips also felt he had taken Elvis as far as he could. The boy was a sensation in the South, but he was practically unknown on a national level. The Colonel knew important people in New York and Hollywood, people who could make Elvis a star from coast to coast.

Except for a brief visit in December 1956, when he fell into an informal sing-along with Sun stars Carl Perkins, Jerry Lee Lewis, and Johnny Cash, later dubbed "the Million Dollar Quartet," Elvis never sang at Sun again. Sam Phillips gave him these final words of advice: "Look, you know how to do it now, you go over there and don't let anybody tell you—they believe enough in you that they've laid some cold cash down, so you let them know what you feel and what you want to do."

CHAPTER FIVE

ALL SHOOK UP: ELVIS '56

"When I first knew Elvis, he had a million dollars' worth of talent. Now he has a million dollars."

—Colonel Tom Parker

At the beginning of 1956, *Cosmopolitan* magazine asked: "What Is an Elvis Presley?" By the end of 1956, the answer to that question was no longer in doubt, not if you owned a television set or picked up a newspaper or ventured into a store where records or souvenirs were sold.

It's no exaggeration to say that Elvis was *everywhere* in 1956. On the record charts, he rose to the top with breathtaking suddenness. In movie theaters, he made a sensational screen debut. On television (where he made nearly an appearance a month), he created a furor every time he swiveled his hips. His was the name on every teenager's lips.

In many ways, his career reached its peak in 1956, when he was only twenty-one years old. Some critics think that, after this unbelievable year, it was all downhill for

Elvis Presley moved on the stage like no one else, with a charisma that excited some audiences and offended others.

Elvis Presley. In later years, these critics believe, the original raw energy of his music would be bleached out. Wherever you stand on this issue, one fact is certain: Elvis '56 was a peak experience, a high point in the singer's twenty-three-year career—and in the history of rock 'n' roll.

Colonel Tom Parker was a man with a plan. A *master* plan. He wanted Elvis to keep reaching bigger and broader audiences, until he eventually became a mainstream, nationwide star. To do that, Parker and the executives at RCA figured, Elvis had to break away from country music, which generally was popular only in the South, and embrace rock 'n' roll.

On January 10, 1956 (two days after his twenty-first birthday), Elvis entered the recording studio for the first time as an RCA artist. Even without Sam Phillips in the booth, he looked and sounded confident, and he tore into a new song called "Heartbreak Hotel," the first song he ever recorded that was written just for him.

When they first heard the song, some RCA officials feared their $35,000 investment had been a waste. They were wrong. By the end of March, "Heartbreak Hotel" had sold close to a million copies. For the first time ever, a single song zoomed to the top of all three charts—pop, country, and R&B. It went on to become the number-one-selling pop record of 1956.

Success on the charts was one thing. But Parker knew that if he wanted to transform Elvis from a regional to a national sensation, he had to get mass exposure. He had to get Elvis on television.

In 1956, television was still something of a novelty. It had, however, entered the homes of most middle-class Americans. Parker knew that in a single television appearance, Elvis could reach more people than he could in months of "Grand Ole Opry"s or "Louisiana Hayride"s.

On January 28, he made his television debut on "Stage Show," a CBS variety program hosted by a pair of big-band musicians named Jimmy and Tommy Dorsey. He was introduced as "a young fellow who . . . came out of nowhere to be an overnight big star. We think tonight," the announcer added, "that he's going to make television history for you." Elvis bounded out and launched into

"Shake, Rattle and Roll," a blues number originally recorded by Big Joe Turner. And shake, rattle, and roll he did! During the instrumental break he cut loose, twisting and twitching in his now famous fashion. Instead of the teen screams he was accustomed to, the program's live audience greeted him with applause mixed with polite laughter. Overall, though, his television debut was a success.

Elvis appeared with the Dorsey brothers six times between January and March. "Stage Show" was not a very popular program, but each time he appeared the show got better and better ratings, a fact that was not lost on other television hosts.

In April, Elvis was booked to sing on "The Milton Berle Show," a big step up from the Dorsey brothers. Berle was a major star, known as "Mr. Television" for his popularity on the new medium. Elvis, full of energy and confidence, sang his big hit, "Heartbreak Hotel." He also appeared in a comedy skit with the host. Playing Elvis's "twin brother Melvin," Berle danced to Elvis's latest release, "Blue Suede Shoes."

In June, Elvis returned to the Berle show. This time he introduced a new song, "Hound Dog," an R&B number first recorded by Big Mama Thornton. The studio audience responded immediately, encouraging Elvis to take his hip-swiveling even farther. During the final verse, he slowed the tempo and shook his pelvis to the beat in a very suggestive fashion. The audience loved every single rebellious second. Berle scored some of his highest ratings ever.

* * * *

Elvis was riding high after his second triumph on "The Milton Berle Show." In July, he stood atop each of the three record charts—pop ("I Want You, I Need You, I Love You"), R&B ("Heartbreak Hotel"), and country ("I Forgot to Remember to Forget"). "Blue Suede Shoes" was also climbing the charts. But while he was enjoying all this success, a big storm was brewing on the horizon.

Outside of Memphis, Elvis had never received much press. To most of America he was an unknown. The Dorsey and Berle shows, however, changed that. They brought him to the attention of millions—many of whom didn't like what they saw. Television made Elvis a star. It also made him more of a threat. Parents couldn't keep him out of the house; he could hip-swivel his way into every living room. And he did.

The day after Elvis tore into "Hound Dog" on the Berle show, the press tore into him. The *New York Herald Tribune* called him "unspeakably untalented and vulgar." A *New York Times* writer proclaimed, "Mr. Presley has no discernible singing ability." The *New York Daily News* complained that pop music had "reached its lowest depths in the 'grunt and groin' antics of one Elvis Presley. . . . He gave an exhibition that was suggestive and vulgar, tinged with the kind of animalism that should be confined to dives and bordellos."

Looking back, it's hard to understand what all the fuss was about. Compared to today's suggestive lyrics and explicit music videos, Presley's moves seem tame—almost wholesome. But in the 1950s, his hip-thrusting created a storm of controversy. He literally "rocked" the nation with his new kind of singing, his long sideburns, and his swiveling hips.

The criticism of Elvis Presley was far-reaching. Ministers preached sermons about the evils of rock music, declaring that Elvis had sunk to "a new low in spiritual degeneracy." A congressman complained of his "animal gyrations." The city of San Antonio banned rock music from local swimming pools because it "attracted undesirable elements given to practicing their spastic gyrations in abbreviated bathing suits." A judge in Jacksonville threatened to arrest Elvis for "impairing the morals of minors" if he didn't tone down his act. (Elvis tried his best. But when he wiggled a finger during a drum solo, the crowd still went wild.)

The young singer was soon being blamed for everything from juvenile delinquency to drug addiction to race riots. To many adults, the most disturbing thing about his act was its suggestion of sex. He was criticized for his "leer" and his "gleeful wallowing in smut." His wiggling was called "vulgar," "indecent," and "obscene." More than one critic compared him to a striptease artist. A Los Angeles journalist complained that "what Elvis offers is not basically music but a sex act." (When the L.A. police attended his show with cameras, he toned down his motions.)

What was Elvis's reaction to the criticism? He was shocked. He was offended that strangers were judging him without even knowing him. He denied the charges: "I don't do any vulgar movements," he said. "I'm not trying to be sexy. It's just my way of expressing how I feel when I move around." Finally, he took comfort in religion: "I don't mind being controversial. Even Jesus wasn't loved in his day." He told a *New York Times* interviewer that he was "at peace" with his conscience, adding humbly: "If I did think I was bad for people, I would go back to driving a truck."

"When I sang hymns back home with Mom and Pop," he told another reporter, "I stood still and I looked like you feel when you sing a hymn. When I sing this rock 'n' roll, my eyes won't stay open and my legs won't stand still. I don't care what they say, it ain't nasty."

When Elvis appeared on NBC's "The Steve Allen Show" on July 1, 1956, the controversy was in full swing.

The show's host, Steve Allen, was caught in the middle. He knew he needed Presley's star power to win the ratings war against Ed Sullivan, host of the most popular show of the day. But Allen also hated rock 'n' roll music. To get around this dilemma, he concocted a scheme to tone Elvis down. At the beginning of his program that evening, he assured viewers he would present "a show the whole family can watch and enjoy." He then introduced "the *new* Elvis Presley"—who emerged from behind the curtain wearing white tie and tails, gloves, and a top hat. When Elvis performed his new single, "Hound Dog," there was no wiggling, no shaking. This time he sang it standing perfectly still, while a live basset hound listened from a wooden platform, looking bored and confused.

Elvis was a good sport, but he was clearly uncomfortable with this "new Elvis." He wasn't the only one. The next morning, teenage fans picketed NBC, waving signs that read, "We Want the GYRATIN' Elvis."

* * * * *

"Teenagers are my life and my triumph. I'd be nowhere without them."
—Elvis Presley

The more adults denounced Elvis or tried to censor his music, the more teenagers loved him. In their minds Elvis equaled rebellion, and if parents hated him, so much the better. Elvis almost single-handedly created the "Generation Gap," a deep crack in the culture between old and young. After his Steve Allen appearance, *Newsweek* magazine wrote that "civilization today is sharply divided into two schools which cannot stand the sight of each other." It was a war between the parents and the teenagers. And the teenagers were winning.

Teenagers made Elvis a star. They also made him very, very rich. In October, *Variety* magazine announced that, based on record sales, television appearances, and a new deal to star in movies, Elvis Presley was a millionaire. Such a quick windfall was unprecedented in the entertainment business at that time.

The *Variety* report did not include merchandising, a gold mine for Elvis and the Colonel. In the prosperous 1950s, teens had more disposable income than ever before. And how did they choose to dispose of their income? On Elvis merchandise. A teenager with some extra cash could go to the local store and purchase any one (or more) of the following Elvis items: record cases, charm bracelets, dog tags, toy guitars, board games, belts, scarves, skirts, jeans, paste-on sideburns, blue suede shoes, stuffed hound dogs, houndburgers, "Love Me Tender" perfume, or lipstick in "Tutti-Frutti" red, "Heartbreak Hotel" pink, and "Hound Dog" orange. By the end of 1956, seventy-eight different Elvis products had generated $22 million for Elvis Presley Enterprises, Inc.

Let's not forget records. By October Elvis had sold more than ten million singles, making RCA's investment look like the deal of the century.

The day after his Steve Allen appearance, Elvis returned to the studio and recorded "Hound Dog," a song he'd been singing in concert for months (although it took thirty-one takes to record a version that satisfied him). That same day, he searched through a stack of demo tapes and found a song called "Don't Be Cruel," which he recorded before dinner. "Hound Dog," with "Don't Be Cruel" on the flip side, wound up the number-two record of 1956. It was a costly mistake for RCA, which almost certainly could have doubled its money by releasing the popular songs on two separate 45's.

Between television appearances and recording sessions, Elvis returned to the road. And as he crisscrossed the country, the frenzy and pandemonium—or *fan*demonium—continued to grow.

Anybody who attended an Elvis concert in 1956 was struck by one thing: the noise. The screams and squeals from his thousands of teenybopper fans were enough to pierce the toughest eardrum. They "sounded like fifty jet

Elvis in a contemplative moment during the recording of "Hound Dog"

planes taking off at once," according to a Canadian newspaper. In Detroit, a reporter called the experience "the closest thing to getting bashed in the head with an atomic bomb." At a Memphis concert, the roar was so loud that patients at four nearby hospitals were given extra sleeping pills. Scotty Moore used to say that the screams were so loud, he and Bill and D. J. Fontana (a new drummer added to the band in 1955) couldn't hear the music; they had to follow Elvis's gyrating backside just to keep in tempo.

Sometimes the fan reaction was amusing. Other times it was downright scary. In New Orleans, fans tied up an elevator operator and kidnapped Elvis inside an elevator. In Hawaii they attacked him as he walked to his car, taking his shirt, ring, watch, and wallet. In Kansas City there was a full-scale riot; D. J.'s drums and Bill's bass were smashed, and D. J. himself was tossed into the orchestra pit.

And so it went. There was more hysteria every week as the Elvis road show moved from town to town. In Dallas he attracted a crowd of twenty-six thousand, a record for that city. In Tupelo, his hometown, the National Guard was called in to protect him from thousands of crying teenagers. At a charity concert in Memphis, his other hometown, Elvis told the screaming crowd that "those people in New York are not gonna change me none. I'm gonna show you what the real Elvis is like tonight."

How was "the real Elvis" handling the hysteria? Unfortunately, he had trouble getting away from it. His fans surrounded him, even at the new house he had bought for his parents in Memphis. Not that they weren't polite. They were just *there*, every single day, standing by the carport, waiting for Elvis to come out and sign autographs. They pressed stethoscopes against the walls, hoping to hear him snore. They plucked blades of grass from the yard as a token of admission to local fan clubs. (Vernon hardly ever had to mow the lawn.) To feed the crowds, vendors set up wagons outside the home and sold hot dogs and ice cream. On hot days Gladys sent ice water to the thirsty fans.

Not everybody in Memphis, however, was so polite. When Elvis stopped for gas at a local filling station, his fans created a disturbance and he ended up in a fistfight with the manager. The event made all the papers. Elvis kept going out; he didn't want to be a prisoner in his home. Even a simple trip to the movies ended in a near-riot as fans surrounded his Cadillac and tore it apart. "It's getting where I can't even leave the house without something happening to me," he said.

Stardom was all Elvis had ever wanted. But stardom was leaving him all shook up. It took a physical toll: in February he collapsed after a concert in Jacksonville. Elvis said the doctor told him that "I was doing as much work in twenty minutes as the average laborer does in eight hours. He said if I didn't slow up, I'd have to lay off a couple of years."

The success also started affecting his mental state. In 1956 he told a friend he was "lonesome" at the top. "I'm afraid," he said to a reporter. "I'm afraid I'll go out like a light, just like I came on." The night of his Steve Allen appearance, he told an interviewer named Hy Gardner that he was having trouble sleeping. "Everything has happened to me so fast during the last year and a half," he confessed. "I'm all mixed up, you know? I can't keep up with everything that's happened."

Who could blame him? Such a meteoric rise to the top was unprecedented. He had never had any money, and suddenly he was a millionaire. He'd always been a loner, and suddenly, at just twenty-one years of age, he was followed by thousands of screaming fans.

He would say later of his astounding success:

I don't know what it is. I just fell into it, really. My daddy and I were laughing about it the other day. He looked at me and said, "What happened, El? The last thing I can remember is I was working in a can factory and you were driving a truck." We all feel the same way about it still. It just . . . caught us up.

*****

Elvis's amazing year ended where it began: on television.

Early in 1956, popular television host Ed Sullivan said of Elvis, "He'll never appear on my show." That was before "The Ed Sullivan Show" was beaten in the ratings by Elvis's appearance on "The Steve Allen Show"—a rare defeat for Sullivan, whose show was the highest-rated variety program on the air. Eventually, he agreed to pay Elvis $50,000 for three appearances on "The Ed Sullivan Show." (Only weeks earlier, the Colonel had asked for $5,000 a show and Sullivan had turned him down.)

On September 9, Elvis appeared on the first Sullivan show of the 1956–57 season, singing four numbers, including "Don't Be Cruel" and his new single, "Love Me Tender." It seemed as if everybody in America was watching. The show reached 82.6 percent of the television audience, the greatest numbers in ratings history. Based on this phenomenal reception, record stores ordered nearly a million copies of "Love Me Tender" before it was even released.

During his third and final appearance on "The Ed Sullivan Show," on January 6, 1957, something unusual happened: he was seen only from the waist up. Afraid that Elvis's pelvis would corrupt America's youth, the CBS censors ordered the cameramen not to shoot his wiggling hips (although the screams of the studio audience let television viewers know that *something* was going on down there). On a more wholesome note, Elvis thanked the audience for the 282 teddy bears they had sent him for Christmas. Afterward, Sullivan declared Elvis to be "a real decent, fine boy" and "a very nice person."

The appearances on "The Ed Sullivan Show" were the culmination of an amazing year. No longer just a regional phenomenon, Elvis was now a sensation from coast to coast.

Elvis Presley's appearance on
"The Ed Sullivan Show" in 1956 helped
establish him as a national star.

CHAPTER SIX

—— ELVIS ——
GOES TO HOLLYWOOD, PART I

"Singers come and go, but if you're a good actor, you can last a long time."

—Elvis Presley

Elvis loved movies. As a kid he haunted the local theaters, hoarding his nickels for double features. In high school, as an usher at Loew's State Theater in Memphis, he got paid to watch his favorite films again and again. All his life he wanted to be an actor like his heroes, James Dean and Marlon Brando. He studied their every move and mannerism and even memorized every line of Dean's most famous film, *Rebel Without a Cause*. Even when he was a nationwide rock 'n' roll sensation, Elvis longed to be a movie star.

Elvis certainly had plenty of charisma for the big screen—a fact that was not lost on Hal Wallis, a well-known movie producer. Early in 1956, Wallis happened to see Elvis shake up the audience on the Dorseys' "Stage Show." One glimpse of those screaming teenagers and Wallis knew he was looking at box-office gold.

On April 1, 1956, Wallis brought the teen idol to Hollywood for a screen test. While cameras rolled, Elvis sang "Blue Suede Shoes," then performed a couple of scenes from a popular play, *The Rainmaker*. Though he had never acted before, he was no April fool. "I got out there and just tried to put myself in the place of the character I was playing," he said, "just trying to act as naturally as I could."

Wallis was pleased. "When I ran the test I felt the same thrill I experienced when I first saw Errol Flynn [a 1930s and '40s movie star] on the screen," he said. "Elvis, in a very different, modern way, had exactly the same power, virility, and sexual drive. The camera caressed him." After an intense negotiation with the Colonel, Wallis agreed to pay Elvis $450,000 for a three-picture deal.

His first movie, originally titled *The Reno Brothers*, was a drama about four southern brothers who are chased by Union troops after the Civil War. Elvis played the youngest brother, which was not the leading role. It was the first and only time he appeared in a movie that did not feature him in the starring role. He sang four songs, including "Love Me Tender," the ballad he had introduced on "The Ed Sullivan Show." When the song rocketed up the charts, the producers wisely changed the movie's title to *Love Me Tender*.

Although he told one of his costars he was "plenty scared," Elvis worked hard and the director was pleased with his performance. The only hitch occurred when it was announced that Elvis would die at the end of the film. Angry fans picketed the front of New York's Paramount Theater with signs reading "Don't Die! Elvis Presley." Although some cynics thought the protest was a publicity stunt engineered by the Colonel, the movie's producers quickly shot a new ending that softened the blow.

A still from *Love Me Tender*, in which Elvis played a farmer during the Civil War

Love Me Tender was released on November 15, 1956. Reviews were generally dreadful. A *Time* magazine critic said Elvis had all the star power of a sausage. *Variety* wrote, "Appraising Presley as an actor, he ain't. Not that it makes any difference."

On the latter point, *Variety* was right. The premiere drew one of the largest crowds in movie history. When the Paramount Theater doors opened for the 8 A.M. show, there were fifteen hundred teenagers waiting patiently in line. Thanks to his legions of fans, Elvis's first movie did record-setting business. Only twenty-one years old, he was well on his way to achieving movie-star status.

By the beginning of 1957, Elvis Presley had an image that was known to the whole world. He was the snarling rebel, the devilish dynamo. He had earned the title "Elvis the Pelvis" for his hip-swiveling moves. He was the number-one threat to American teenagers. In a word, Elvis was *dangerous*.

Colonel Tom Parker considered Elvis's rebel image a major problem. In order to generate as much money as possible, the Colonel couldn't rely solely on the fickle teen market. He had to figure out a way for Elvis to appeal to adults as well as teenagers; he had to bridge the Generation Gap. The Colonel had to stop Elvis from playing the rebel and prove to the world that Elvis was a decent young man.

So, in 1956 and 1957, certain newspaper and magazine articles—planted, of course, by the Colonel—started depicting a nice, innocent kid named Elvis Presley, who loved his mama and who never smoked or drank (statements that were both true). This "new" Elvis said he was confused by his success, and tried to distance himself from the controversy he generated. He started promoting charities like the March of Dimes. In a 1956 article entitled "Halo, Everybody, Halo," *Variety* magazine reported that "there is talk of accenting Presley's church-going family background," in order to "re-create the rock 'n' roller into an influence for the good."

At the Colonel's insistence, the "new" Elvis also passed up movies about rock 'n' roll rebels to shoot his second movie: a wholesome picture called *Loving You*.

Loving You was loosely based on Presley's life (or the life the Colonel wanted fans to believe). He played Deke Rivers, a truck driver turned musician who doesn't fit in with the country music scene. Pushed by his ruthless manager (played by Lizabeth Scott), this southern boy tours the country, whipping up a frenzy in every town he visits—and is criticized for being a dangerous influence on the nation's teenagers. In the end, Deke proves he's been misunderstood.

With seven musical numbers, *Loving You* goes a long way toward capturing the energy and the frenzy of Elvis in concert. (Look closely at the audience for Deke's final performance and you'll spot Gladys and Vernon.) The *Loving You* soundtrack consists of authentic rock 'n' roll, backed by Scotty and Bill. The album reached number one on some charts and generated two hit singles, the title song and "Teddy Bear." The movie also succeeded at the box office. For his next picture Elvis was offered not only $250,000 up front, but also 50 percent of the movie's eventual profits, a deal that *Time* magazine said was "unheard of."

Elvis's third movie, *Jailhouse Rock*, was also designed to polish his new image, though this time a bit of the old rebel manages to shine through. Again his character is rough on the outside but softhearted underneath. Again he plays a musician, Vince Everett, who learns to sing and play the guitar when he's sent to prison for killing a man in self-defense. By the time he gets out, he's an angry young man whose voice and animal magnetism make him a rock star. An accident softens his hard edges, and in the end he falls in love with the heroine.

Jailhouse Rock is a low-budget film shot in black and white. Many critics think it's the best movie Elvis ever made. His performance is gritty, raw, and passionate. One review carried the headline "Elvis Can Act!" The title song—written by Jerry Lieber and Mike Stoller, who also wrote "Hound Dog" and "Loving You"—is a hard-rocking number that went to number one before the movie was even released. Elvis also got a chance to show off his dancing skills. His rendition of "Jailhouse Rock" is a red-hot number that features Elvis (and a cast of professional dancers) cutting loose, twisting and gyrating, and sliding down a pole.

Elvis was serious about his movie career. Every night he studied his performance in the scenes shot that day (much as he used to study his idols, Brando and Dean). "I always criticize myself in films," he said. "I'm always striving to be natural in front of a camera. That takes studying, of a sort."

One thing he learned from his studies was to never smile. He told a reporter:

I've made a study of Marlon Brando. I've made a study of poor Jimmy Dean. I've made a study of myself, and I know why girls go for us. We're sullen, we're broodin', we're something of a menace. . . . I don't know anything about Hollywood, but I know you can't be sexy if you smile. You can't be a rebel if you grin.

His colleagues praised him as a hard worker. The assistant director of *Jailhouse Rock* said he was "dedicated and focused" on his work. He never did take acting

Elvis dances with other inmates in a production number from the movie *Jailhouse Rock*.

lessons, however. "It wouldn't hurt me any to go to [acting] school," he admitted after *Love Me Tender*. "But I learn best by experience. I never was very good in schools of any kind." Still, his acting improved greatly over the course of his first three movies. Many in Hollywood felt he had the potential for a long, successful career on the screen.

* * * *

In March 1957, Elvis bought a second house in Memphis, quite amazing for a twenty-two-year-old who had grown up in a federal housing project.

This house was a real stunner, even more impressive than the first. (Incidentally, a candy company offered to buy the paneling from Elvis's first house; they wanted to cut it up and give away the pieces in packages of bubble gum. In a rare case of restraint, the Colonel said no.) Surrounded by tall oak trees and 14 acres (5.7 ha) of rolling countryside, the eighteen-room house was very much in the southern style, a mansion with a white-columned patio. It was named Graceland, after a relative of the original owners, and it cost Elvis more than $100,000.

Elvis had big plans for Graceland. He eventually spent another $500,000 remodeling the house, adding an 8-foot (2.4-m) stone fence, a swimming pool, even a working soda fountain where he and his friends could get a milk shake whenever they wanted. Gladys planted a garden out back; it reminded her of Mississippi. One day Elvis drove out to the country and returned with a Cadillac full of chickens, geese, ducks, and peacocks for the yard. The ducks made themselves at home in the pool.

Life at Graceland was never dull. The place was always crawling with uncles, aunts, cousins, friends, and friends of friends. Elvis organized football games and roller-skating parties. He and his pals rode horses and motorcycles and played badminton in the yard.

Elvis continued to have plenty of uninvited guests, too. Although he bought Graceland to give his family more privacy, his fans still gathered outside the front gates (which were decorated with musical notes and two guitar-playing figures). Day and night they stood there, waiting for Elvis to drive through the gates, hoping he would stop to chat or sign an autograph. The fans were a constant presence. When the Memphis police got a

Elvis in front of Graceland,
his Memphis mansion

report about a teenage runaway, the first place they checked was Graceland.

* * * *

By the end of 1957, Elvis had achieved success beyond—or at least equal to—his wildest dreams. But he started paying a price for that success. His fans continued to cause a commotion when he ventured out into the world. Never again would he be able to hang out in public like a normal twenty-two-year-old. If he wanted to buy some new clothes, he had to make arrangements to shop after the store was closed. If he wanted to see a movie, he had to rent out the entire theater for a private midnight showing.

"It's lonesome," he told a friend at the peak of his popularity. When the friend asked how someone could be lonesome when thousands of people adored him and followed his every move, Elvis replied, "Well, I can't go get a hamburger, I can't go in some greasy little joint, I can't go water skiing or shopping."

The Colonel contributed to his isolation by sheltering him from the outside world. He told Elvis whom he should spend time with and whom he should make music with. When Scotty Moore and Bill Black, his original band mates, complained that they were being cut out of Elvis's career, the Colonel let them quit. Although Elvis eventually hired them back, things between them were never the same. It's easy to see how Elvis Presley could have felt trapped—trapped by the Colonel's demands, by the expectations of his fans, and by the burdens of his success.

CHAPTER SEVEN

—— PRIVATE ——
PRESLEY

"Elvis died when he went into the Army."

—John Lennon

Colonel Tom Parker's campaign to tame Elvis the rebel—
to create the image of a wholesome, all-American boy
who could be loved equally by teenagers and parents—
was given an unexpected boost at the end of 1957. Just
before Christmas, Elvis received a draft notice ordering
him to join the U.S. Army.

Elvis was nervous about joining the service. He
feared his career would screech to a halt, that his fans
would find another teen idol to worship. Publicly,
though, he stated that he was eager to do his patriotic
duty. "I'll do what I have to do—like any American boy,"
he declared. The Colonel made a point of telling
reporters how much money (millions and millions of dollars!) Elvis was giving up to serve his country.

Elvis was supposed to be inducted into the Army in

January 1958. But producer Hal Wallis and Paramount Pictures asked for a two-month deferment so he could finish shooting his fourth movie, *King Creole*. Elvis again plays a singer with a wild, new sound. He gets involved with gangsters, battles hoodlums on the street, and wins the leading woman and redeems himself. Director Michael Curtiz, who had made *Casablanca, Angels with Dirty Faces*, and other classics, was a strict taskmaster, and Elvis worked hard to meet his demands. When Curtiz told him he was too heavy for the role, Elvis shed 10 pounds (4.5 kg) in two weeks. The hard work paid off. His performance in *King Creole* earned some of the best reviews of his career.

On March 24, 1958, Elvis Presley reported for Army duty in Memphis. If he was nervous or upset, he did a good job of covering it. He told reporters that his stint in the Army would be "a great experience. The Army can do anything it wants with me. Millions of other guys have been drafted, and I don't want to be different from anyone else." Although he was offered a job in the Special Services, where he would have simply performed for the Army's brass, he refused any kind of special treatment. He wanted to be seen as a regular GI.

It was no surprise to anyone that Elvis's induction into the Army was greeted with the usual hysteria. More than two dozen reporters, including some from England, waited for him at the induction center. The crowd swelled to more than fifty when his famous hair was cut off—the most photographed haircut in history. ("Hair today, gone tomorrow," Elvis joked.) When he was eventually assigned to the Second Armored Division at Fort Hood, Texas, a convoy of fans and reporters followed his bus more than 200 miles (322 km); there was a small riot at every rest stop.

After his first day at Fort Hood, the Army kicked out all the reporters and photographers. Suddenly, for the

Elvis Presley gives his mother a farewell kiss on the eve of his induction into the Army.

first time in nearly three years, Elvis was no longer the center of attention, no longer the internationally known actor and singer. He was simply Private Presley, free to settle into the routine of a U.S. soldier.

* * * *

Five months into boot camp, Elvis received the shock of his young life. A Memphis doctor called to tell him that his mother had collapsed at Graceland and been taken to the hospital. Her condition was critical.

Elvis, on emergency leave from the Army, and his father visit his ailing mother in a Memphis hospital.

Gladys Presley had been ailing for some time. She ate poorly, drank too much, and took too many diet pills. (As the mother of a sex symbol, she had become self-conscious about her weight.) Her psychological health was also unsteady. Her son's sudden fame had filled her with fear. She cringed whenever she saw fans lunge for him onstage. She also worried about his safety in the Army—they had never been apart for more than a few weeks at a time. In fact, Elvis moved his parents to Texas to be closer to him. But his mother's health continued to worsen, and she returned to Memphis.

Elvis followed her home on August 12. (He had to fight for an emergency leave because the Army didn't want to appear to favor Private Presley.) He rushed to her bedside and arranged to have her favorite pink Cadillac parked outside her hospital window. Her spirits were lifted, but not for long. Gladys Presley died on August 14, 1958, of a heart attack brought on by acute hepatitis. She was forty-six.

Her funeral was another media circus. Three thousand people viewed the body at the Memphis Funeral Home. (More than a hundred thousand fans sent cards and letters.) Sixty-five policemen controlled the crowds outside. Even during this emotional time, Elvis was constantly surrounded by the press.

At the funeral, he broke down in front of all those fans and photographers. His grieving was almost impossible to watch. He threw himself on her coffin. He caressed her body and combed her hair. He talked to her, using the pet names they had always used. He collapsed several times during the service. "Everything I have is gone," he sobbed at the cemetery. "I lived my whole life for you!" Said one observer, "I have never seen a man suffer as much or grieve as much as he did at the loss of his mother."

Losing the source of his confidence devastated Elvis. "His mother had been the one," said writer Stanley Booth, "perhaps the only one, who had told him throughout his life that even though he came from poor country people, he was just as good as anyone."

Now his champion, his protector, his security was

gone—a fact he seemed unable to believe. After the funeral he ordered that her clothes be left in her closet, and that a pane of glass she broke when she collapsed be left unfixed. For many years he kept the artificial tree from their last Christmas together. And he never gave up that pink Cadillac. It was the one car he kept his whole life.

* * * *

Still sick with grief, Elvis returned to Texas. Then, on September 22, 1958, his unit was shipped overseas to an Army post in Friedberg, West Germany. While 125 newsmen watched and an Army band played "All Shook Up," his ship sailed from New York. Aboard ship he consoled himself with a book, *Poems That Touch the Heart,* which included a poem called "Mother."

In Germany, Elvis was a member of the Thirty-second Tank Battalion. He took part in maneuvers close to the border of Czechoslovakia (then part of the Communist bloc). For his labors he earned $78 a month, a slight pay cut from the estimated $400,000 a month he was making back in the States.

By most accounts he got along well with the other soldiers. Earlier, he had been the subject of some ribbing. "Miss your teddy bears, Elvis?" somebody might shout, or "Boy, you ain't wiggling right!" But eventually, when they saw him pull kitchen duty like any recruit, they accepted this millionaire superstar as one of their own.

He had never been so far from home, and now that Gladys was gone he missed his family more than ever. To keep him company he brought his father, Vernon; his grandmother, Minnie Mae; and a couple of Memphis buddies, Red West (a Humes High School football star) and Lamar Fike to Germany. They rented a modest house at 14 Goethestrasse in the nearby town of Bad Nauheim. Elvis visited whenever he wasn't on duty. To make the place seem more like home, he stocked the refrigerator with his favorite American foods, like bacon and hamburger patties, and he bought a television and a piano. He sometimes invited his fellow soldiers home for sing-alongs.

In Germany, Elvis began his lifelong love affair with karate. One of the country's leading instructors visited his house three or four times a week to give him private lessons. Eventually Elvis qualified for an eighth-level black belt.

Even in Germany (where he was called the "rock 'n' roll matador"), he found himself at the center of attention. He still had a tough time venturing out in public. When he attended a Bill Haley and the Comets concert in nearby Frankfurt, he was asked to stay in Haley's dressing room during the show so he wouldn't provoke a riot. Even at his rented house he was surrounded by fans. They traveled from all over Europe, and beyond, to get a glimpse of their idol. Eventually he was forced to post a sign in the front window: "Autographs between seven-thirty and eight-thirty P.M." (although he often chatted and mingled well past the deadline).

Germany was the site of two important meetings for the Presley men. Vernon got to know a woman named Dee Stanley, whom he married in 1960. And Elvis met a young woman—a girl, actually—named Priscilla Beaulieu.

The stepdaughter of an Air Force major stationed in Germany, Priscilla was introduced to Elvis by a mutual friend in 1959. (There's a story that when she told her stepfather she wanted to meet Elvis, he replied that he wouldn't let her walk across the street to see him.) They dated often during his last few months in Germany, usually spending time with his family at the Bad Nauheim house. Priscilla—or "Cilla," as Elvis called her—was only fourteen years old when they met. Although she was sometimes photographed with Elvis, the media rarely commented on his infatuation with such a young girl. At

Priscilla Beaulieu was just fourteen years old when she first met Elvis Presley during his tour of duty in Germany.

a press conference back in the United States, he was careful to downplay the situation. Asked if he had left any girlfriends behind in Germany, he replied: "Not any special ones." By keeping his relationship with Priscilla under wraps, Elvis was able to avoid a major controversy.

Elvis spent seventeen months in Germany, earning his sergeant's stripes. When his tour of duty ended on March 5, 1960, he flew back to Memphis.

What awaited him back home? Colonel Tom Parker was gearing up to promote the more mature (and more patriotic) Elvis. Wisely, the Colonel had figured out a way to keep his client in the public eye—even though he was thousands of miles away. He had stockpiled enough material for several records to be released while Elvis was in the Army (and on a furlough, Elvis had recorded another five songs). Also, *King Creole* had not come out until several months after his induction.

Still, Elvis worried that his career would fizzle after his two-year hitch in the Army. He knew how quickly he had risen to the top—and he feared that just as quickly he could fall back down to earth. "It's all over," he told a friend before he returned to the States. "They aren't going to know me when I get back."

CHAPTER EIGHT

ELVIS GOES TO HOLLYWOOD, PART II

> *"I'll play it my way—nice, clean, wholesome."*
> —Elvis Presley as Tulsa McLean
> in *G.I. Blues*, a 1960 movie

The world Elvis returned to in 1960 was very different from the one he left in 1958. His mother was dead. His father had remarried. His fans had changed, too. When the president of one of his fan clubs visited him, he hardly recognized her. "She's going to college now," he said. "I was surprised she looked me up. She was more mature, but she stopped by anyway."

Elvis himself was a changed man. For one thing, he no longer had a record on the charts or a hit movie in the theaters. But he wasted no time getting his career back on track. Two weeks after his release from the Army, he was in the studio recording an album for RCA. It quickly became apparent that his fears of a career setback were pointless. Even before he finished it, one million orders had been placed for the new album, appropriately called *Elvis Is Back*.

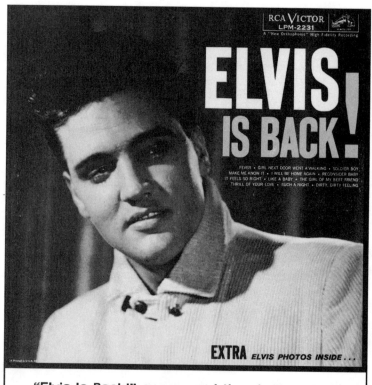

"Elvis Is Back!" announced the singer's first album after his return from the Army.

He may have been back, but he sure didn't sound the same. By 1960 the Colonel was even more anxious to distance Elvis from rock 'n' roll. The music he helped invent had become more controversial than ever. Famous rocker Chuck Berry had been arrested for having sex with a minor, while Jerry Lee Lewis (a Sun Records artist) shocked the country by marrying his fourteen-year-old cousin. The Colonel wanted Elvis to have no part of this scandalous world.

So when Elvis recorded *Elvis Is Back*, which hit the

stores only two months after he left the Army, he started moving into the mainstream. He moved away from rock to pop, to music that was more acceptable to an adult audience. Despite a few bluesy numbers like "Reconsider Baby," the album featured a more mellow sound. In the same session he recorded two ballads, "Are You Lonesome Tonight?" and "It's Now or Never," which were released on later albums. Both became number-one hits. "It's Now or Never" sold a whopping nine million copies. Elvis the rebel was gradually becoming Elvis the ballad singer, a crooner like his teenage idol Dean Martin.

Outside the studio, Elvis received praise for interrupting his career to serve his country. On the floor of the U.S. Congress, where three years earlier a congressman had complained of his "animal gyrations," Senator Estes Kefauver read a tribute to Sergeant Presley, which was printed in the *Congressional Record*. The media also took note of the new image. Wrote *Life* magazine in 1960:

> *The Elvis Presley everyone thinks he is—isn't. He is no longer the sneering, hip-swinging symbol of the untamed beast that resides in 17-year-old breasts.*

When Elvis returned to television—the medium he rocked with his controversial appearances on the Berle and Sullivan shows—he left the sneer behind. On May 12, 1960, he appeared on "The Frank Sinatra Timex Show." (The deal, worked out months before he left the Army, paid him $150,000, a record-setting fee.) Like Elvis, Sinatra was a singer (from the 1940s) who had made the teenagers swoon but turned to movies and mainstream music as he got older. The Colonel must have seen Sinatra as a perfect model for Elvis's post-Army career.

To show what a patriotic, clean-cut young man he had become, Elvis sang his first number wearing his Army uniform. In other segments he wore a conservative tuxedo. In a duet, Elvis sang Sinatra's hit "Witch-craft" while Sinatra did a rendition of "Love Me Tender." It was a far cry from the hip-swiveling rebel. But the studio audience ate it up. (It didn't hurt that the Colonel packed the house with four hundred members of an Elvis fan club.)

The Sinatra show would be his last television appearance until the end of 1968. For the next eight years, if you wanted to see Elvis perform, you had to go to the movies.

* * * *

"He's the best-mannered star in Hollywood and he . . . has a determination to be a fine actor. He was smart enough to simmer down that torrid act of his."
—journalist Hedda Hopper

Elvis was eager to get back to Hollywood. He had not forgotten his dream of becoming a movie star. Indeed, he sometimes talked as though his acting were more important than his singing: "I don't know how long the music end of it will last," he said.

Like his early films, his first movie after the Army reflected his personal life. *G.I. Blues* tells the story of a young American GI, a member of a tank division stationed in Germany, who loves to sing and chase girls.

Unlike those first movies, however, *G.I. Blues* had not even a hint of the 1950s rebel image. Elvis's hair is short. (The pre-Army ducktail would never return.) Although he shakes his hips a little, they never swivel. His girl-chasing is downright wholesome. In one scene he takes his love interest to a puppet show, in another he baby-sits for an adorable little baby. *G.I. Blues* was nothing more than a light musical comedy—fun for the whole family.

The transformation worked. The movie was a hit, the fourteenth most popular film of 1960. (It also caused a sensation in other countries. When fans rioted in a Mexico City theater, the movie was banned in the entire country.) The soundtrack, featuring a new version of his 1956 hit "Blue Suede Shoes," stayed at number one longer than any of his previous albums.

Elvis still wanted to be taken seriously as an actor. For his next two pictures, he would get his way. *Flaming Star* (1960) had actually been written for one of his idols, Marlon Brando. It was a serious drama about a serious topic: racial prejudice. Elvis played the son of a white father and an American Indian mother who is trapped in the middle of a small-town race war. *Wild in the Country* (1961) was scripted by a famous Broadway playwright, Clifford Odets. It tells the story of a young hothead who falls in love with a psychologist, discovers a talent for writing, and eventually goes to college.

Despite respectful reviews for Elvis's performances, neither serious film was a commercial hit. In fact, the readers of *Teen* magazine voted Elvis and his *Wild in the Country* costar, Tuesday Weld, the Damp Raincoat Award for Most Disappointing Performers of 1961.

Neither picture could compete at the box office with his next movie, *Blue Hawaii*. In this entertaining bit of fluff, Elvis plays a rich young playboy, the heir to a pineapple fortune, who would rather romp on the beach than join the family business. (Elvis had to overcome a fear of deep water to film these scenes.) Only when he proves that he can make it on his own as a tourist guide does he return to the warm embrace of his family.

Unlike *Flaming Star* and *Wild in the Country, Blue Hawaii* was a lighthearted musical comedy. It featured fourteen songs, including the hit ballad "Can't Help Falling in Love." Elvis fans got to see their boy swimming, singing, dancing, and romancing. As a result, the movie was a runaway hit, grossing almost $5 million—Elvis's most successful ever.

*****

With *Blue Hawaii*, the Colonel and producer Hal Wallis had devised a winning—that is to say, a moneymaking—formula. The Colonel would stick to this formula almost exclusively for another eight years and twenty-three movies. He and Presley had invented a new motion-picture genre: the Elvis Movie.

The recipe for an Elvis Movie had essentially seven ingredients: (1) Send Elvis to an exotic locale, preferably one with a beach (Hawaii, Acapulco, Fort Lauderdale). (2) Surround him with lots of beautiful, bikini-clad girls. (3) Give him a racy convertible sports car and an unusual, glamorous job (boxer, pilot, race-car driver, trapeze artist). (4) Get him involved in a silly plot (Elvis is kidnapped by evil Arabians; Elvis flies a helicopter filled with dogs). (5) Let him get into the occasional fistfight to show that he isn't a sissy and to defend his (or his girl's) honor. (6) Never, ever let Elvis have any serious faults and don't let his fans see him curse, smoke, drink, cheat, or steal. (Or, God forbid, die.) And (7) make sure to let him break into song at any time, at any place (a shower, grass hut, diving board), and for no apparent reason.

In other words, an Elvis Movie was frivolous, nonsensical, and mindless. It was, as one advertisement put it, "Elvis barrelin', bikin', and bikini-ing and belting out the wild Presley beat!" According to writers Jane and Michael Stern, an Elvis Movie consisted of "90 minutes of Elvis goofing around in front of the camera—nothing less, nothing more." You could look at the Elvis Movie as the father of the MTV video. Instead of the plot, it was music and the pretty Technicolor pictures that counted.

Today this formula sounds silly, even dull. In the 1960s, however, it worked like a charm. "A Presley picture," producer Wallis bragged, "is the only sure thing in Hollywood." Another director (slightly jealous, perhaps) disagreed slightly: "There are only *two* surefire things in this business—Walt Disney and Elvis Presley."

True. An Elvis Movie never lost money, as the Colonel was fond of pointing out. In fact, each film averaged a $5 million profit—and cost only one tenth that much to make. Elvis himself profited greatly, earning a million dollars per film plus 50 percent of the profits (plus a percentage of the soundtrack sales). At one point Elvis Presley was the highest-paid actor in Hollywood.

Once Elvis and the Colonel hit on the formula for moneymaking movies, they started cranking them out. Between 1960 and 1969, Elvis averaged nearly three movies a year, a grueling schedule by any standard. For eight years he completely gave up live concerts and television appearances.

As he worked longer and longer hours to make the movies his fans wanted to see, the quality of these movies worsened. By the end of the 1960s, they were so bad that only the most adoring fan could stand to watch them.

* * * *

*"Only thing worse than watching
a bad movie is being in one."*
—Elvis Presley

The two stars of *Kissin' Cousins*, a 1964 comedy, were Elvis Presley and . . . Elvis Presley. In an outrageous twist, Elvis played a pair of cousins: one a blond hillbilly, the other a dark-haired officer who tries to convince the hillbilly to let the Air Force build a nuclear missile silo on his land. Maybe the characters represented two sides of his past—the Army Elvis and the rural Elvis.

Whatever the reason for doubling Elvis, *Kissin' Cousins* was a low point in his career. The plot barely made sense. The hillbilly characters were crude caricatures of Southerners: heavy drinkers, lazy, and barefoot. The music was lame. Because the movie was shot in less than three weeks, there was no time to rehearse the dance numbers. (Producer Sam Katzman was known as the King of the Quickies.) Because the budget was only $800,000 (a mere one fifth of *Blue Hawaii*'s budget), scenes set in the Smoky Mountains of North Carolina were actually filmed in southern California.

Kissin' Cousins was unquestionably an embarrassment. Sadly, it was typical of Elvis's later movies. After 1964, all his films were made with small budgets and short shooting schedules. As the quality dropped off, so did the profits.

There were some exceptions. *Viva Las Vegas* (1964) succeeds because of Elvis's chemistry with costar Ann-Margret, often called "the female Elvis Presley" for her high-energy dancing and her suggestive moves. (Off-screen, she and Elvis shared a brief romance.) The plot is a standard-issue, completely preposterous Elvis Movie. Elvis plays a race-car driver named Lucky Jordan who loses his Las Vegas Grand Prix entry fee down a swimming-pool drain. To regain the money he takes a job as a waiter at the Flamingo Hotel, where he falls in love with the swimming instructor (played by Ann-Margret). Naturally, he wins the money, the race, *and* the girl.

Above-average music (like "What'd I Say," "C'mon Everybody," and the title song) and Ann-Margret's dynamic dancing make this one of Elvis's better films. It set box-office records in Japan and the Philippines, helping to make Elvis a big star in the Far East.

Films like *Viva Las Vegas*, however, were exceptions. Far more typical examples included films like *Girl Happy*, in which a Chicago gangster hires Elvis to spy on his cute

Ann-Margret and Elvis heated up the screen in
Viva Las Vegas, released in 1964.

daughter, even though Elvis plays a singer, not a private detective. (This 1965 movie features one of Elvis's all-time worst tunes, "Do the Clam," a song that was supposed to convince everyone in America to do a dance step called the Clam. It didn't.) Or *Fun in Acapulco*, starring Elvis as a trapeze artist turned lifeguard who overcomes his fear of heights by jumping into the ocean from a 130-foot (40-m) cliff. (Although the outside scenes were shot in Mexico, Elvis filmed all his scenes on a studio lot in Hollywood.) Or *Live a Little, Love a Little*, featuring Elvis as a photographer chased by a man-crazy woman and her 200-pound (91-kg) Great Dane. ("Watch Elvis Click With All These Chicks," read the movie ad.)

As bland as these movies were, the movie soundtracks were even more forgettable. Instead of raw rock 'n' roll numbers like "Jailhouse Rock" and "Blue Suede Shoes," Elvis wasted his talents on silly, throwaway tunes like "No Room to Rhumba in a Sports Car," "Yoga Is as Yoga Does," and "Queenie Wahine's Papaya."

The songs were mediocre because, ironically, Elvis made more money that way. The Colonel had signed a deal with a music publishing company called Hill and Range. Anytime Elvis recorded a song written by a Hill and Range composer, he got not only the performer's royalty but also a share of the publishing royalty. So, rather than lose money by hiring a top songwriter, Elvis used the hacks in the Hill and Range stable.

After 1964, the Colonel decided that Elvis would release nothing but soundtrack albums. Churned out in two or three all-night sessions, they were often poorly produced. As bad as they were, they still sold well, so RCA had no incentive to change the system.

The years in Hollywood nearly destroyed Elvis's music career. By the end of the 1960s, he had lost his stranglehold on the charts. Between 1962's "Good Luck Charm" and 1969's "Suspicious Minds," he had no number-one hit singles. The *Roustabout* soundtrack in 1964 would be his last number-one album for eight years. In 1966 he could place only one song in the top twenty. In 1967 he placed none.

Did Elvis know how bad the movies and soundtracks had gotten? He must have. In the 1950s he had walked out of a movie called *The King and I* because he thought musicals were silly. Now he was starring in movies that were ten times sillier than that award-winning film. "I feel like an idiot breaking into a song while I'm talking to some chick on a train," he once admitted. Later in his movie career he said, "I'm tired of playing a guy who would be in a fight and would start singing to the guy he was beating up." Referring to the exotic locales of his movies, he mockingly called them "Presley travelogues." There were reports toward the end of the movie years that showing up on a film set actually made him physically ill.

Why then did he stay in Hollywood? Why did he let his career get so far off track? The answers to these complicated questions lead back to Presley's legendary manager, Colonel Tom Parker.

* * * *

*"I'd rather try and close a deal
with the devil."*
—Hal Wallis on Colonel Tom
Parker

Complicated, shrewd, manipulative, and *masterful* are all words used to describe the Colonel. Surely stronger, more unprintable words have also been applied to this controversial figure, whom many fans blame for the downturn in Elvis's career.

The Colonel's past has always been a mystery. Key facts were unknown for years. It was not learned until after Elvis's death that the Colonel was not even a U.S.

citizen. He was not Thomas Parker from West Virginia, but Andreas van Kujik from Holland. And he was not an actual colonel; the title was honorary, granted to him by the governor of Tennessee.

One thing is certain: the Colonel loved to make money. He *lived* to make money. He was a smart businessman who knew how to make a deal. For example, although Elvis never wrote a single song, writers often had to agree to share credit (and part of the money) with Elvis as a cowriter before he would record a number.

The Colonel made sure that he benefited from these deals, too. His exclusive contract gave him an unprecedented 25 percent of everything Elvis made. After 1967, a new contract gave him *half* of Elvis's earnings.

The Colonel was a salesman and Elvis was his product. And as early as 1957 he knew Elvis would be a more profitable product after a few rough edges were smoothed away. As critic Jay Cocks wrote, "The Colonel was constantly nudging Presley away from rock, stuffing him into an entertainment package that offered a little something for everyone."

When it came to Elvis's movie career, the Colonel steered him away from the controversial rebel image of his first few films. And once this new formula started working, the Colonel saw no reason to mess with a good thing. Noting in 1966 that every one of Elvis's movies turned a profit, he said, "How do you argue with this kind of success? It's like telling Maxwell House to change their coffee formula when the stuff is selling like no tomorrow."

When Elvis complained about the declining quality of his movies, the Colonel pointed out that Elvis was simply making the movies his fans wanted to see. Elvis had tried serious films, like *Flaming Star* and *Wild in the Country*, and the fans stayed away. No, Parker argued, people wanted to see Elvis singing in fluffy comedies.

They wanted him to play wholesome, virtuous characters who never had any major flaws.

And so the Colonel—who had complete control over Elvis's choice of material—turned down more interesting roles that would have explored Elvis's acting abilities. Barbra Streisand offered him the part of an alcoholic has-been in *A Star Is Born*; the Colonel said no. When director Norman Taurog (who made *Blue Hawaii*) said he wanted Elvis to star in a film as a cold-blooded killer, the Colonel must have shuddered before turning him down.

In 1963 it was announced that Elvis was taking the part of country singer Hank Williams in the movie biography *Your Cheatin' Heart*. For a man who grew up listening to Williams on the "Grand Ole Opry," it would have been a fascinating choice. But this too never came to pass.

At some point in the 1960s, Elvis must have given up on his dream of being the next Brando or James Dean. Earlier in his career he had worked hard on his acting, asking to reshoot scenes even after the director was satisfied. By the end, he simply showed up and did what the director—and the Colonel—told him to do.

Why didn't Elvis stand up to the Colonel? One outrageous theory came from famous rock producer Phil Spector, who was convinced the Colonel had hypnotized Elvis to do his bidding! A more reasonable explanation was that Elvis needed the money. By the end of the 1960s he lived an expensive life, with houses in Memphis and Hollywood, a stable of fancy cars, and many friends and family members on the payroll. The movies paid the bills, and then some.

The Colonel also isolated Elvis from people who could have given him better advice or steered him in a new direction. He made certain that he was the only person in control of Elvis's career.

Finally, Elvis simply didn't like messing with contracts and lawyers and businesspeople. He was intimidated by Hollywood types, whom he considered a bunch of intellectuals. According to Priscilla Beaulieu Presley,

Elvis detested the business side of his career. He would sign a contract without even reading it. . . . When it came time to stand up to the Colonel, he backed off. When [the Colonel] started crossing over the line from business negotiations into Elvis's artistry, Elvis slowly began going downhill.

* * * * *

Priscilla Beaulieu was an up-close witness to Elvis's downhill slide. After his stint in the Army, she returned often to the United States to visit him. In 1962, Elvis persuaded the Beaulieus to let their sixteen-year-old daughter move to Graceland and finish her schooling in Memphis.

For five years she lived with Vernon, his second wife, Dee Stanley, and Elvis—when he wasn't off making movies. It was surely a difficult time for the teenaged Priscilla. For the sake of Elvis's reputation, her presence at Graceland was kept hidden from the press. Elvis controlled her every move, even remaking her in his own image. Her light-brown hair was dyed with the exact shade of black that he used, and swept up into a towering beehive hairdo. In her 1985 book, *Elvis and Me*, Priscilla wrote:

He taught me everything: how to dress, how to walk, how to apply make-up and wear my hair, how to behave, how to return love—his way. Over the years, he became my father, husband, and very nearly God.

Meanwhile Elvis was off in Hollywood, dating his costars and earning a reputation as a ladies' man. When Priscilla picked up local newspapers, she would see headlines like "Elvis Wins Love of Ann-Margret."

On May 1, 1967, Elvis and Priscilla were finally

Elvis and Priscilla cheek to cheek after their 1967 wedding

married at the Aladdin Hotel in Las Vegas, in a private ceremony that included only fourteen people. Exactly nine months later, on February 1, 1968, daughter Lisa Marie Presley was born. Fans sent hundreds of home-made dresses, booties, and blankets.

Lisa Marie was Elvis and Priscilla's only child and was treated like the daughter of a king. Even as a youngster she wore a full-length mink coat and a smiley-face ring with diamonds for eyes. She tooled around the Graceland

**Proud parents with newborn daughter
Lisa Marie**

grounds in her very own customized chrome golf cart.
Elvis was definitely a doting daddy.

His marriage to Priscilla, and the birth of his daughter, marked a period of career rebirth for Elvis. After years of professional mediocrity, he was finally ready to make a stand to save his sinking career.

CHAPTER NINE

—— THE ——
COMEBACK

"Been a long time, baby."
—Elvis Presley on "The '68
Comeback Special"

Elvis was in a bad way by the end of the 1960s. His musical career had fizzled. "Before Elvis," said John Lennon, "there was nothing." By 1968, however, *Elvis* was practically nothing, as far as rock music was concerned. A decade had passed since his last big hit. Bands he influenced and inspired—Lennon's Beatles, the Rolling Stones, the Who, the Doors—had overtaken him in popularity. (When the Beatles debuted on "The Ed Sullivan Show" in 1964, they took away his television ratings record.) These groups were also more ambitious and original. Artistically they were setting the pace.

Elvis's movie career was also losing steam. The long string of mediocre musicals had alienated fans. By the end, the movies were paired with cheesy horror flicks like *Ghidra the Three-Headed Monster* to boost the box office.

They were turning a profit only because they were so cheap to make.

Maybe the worst thing the movies did was turn the King of Rock 'n' Roll into a joker. The Colonel had tried to change his image, to soften the rough edges, but he had gone too far. By the end of 1968, Elvis was more of a square than a rebel.

How could he end his career slump? Elvis and the Colonel decided he should return to the medium where it all got started: television.

**

"They're going to let me do what I want."
—Elvis, introducing "The '68 Comeback Special"

Not surprisingly, though, the Colonel and Elvis had different ideas about what kind of television show he should choose for his comeback.

The Colonel wanted something quick, cheap, and uncontroversial. Specifically, he wanted a Christmas special. In his version, a tuxedo-clad Elvis would step in front of a decorated tree, sing as many traditional Christmas carols as he could squeeze into an hour, wish everyone in the audience a happy holiday, and exit.

Elvis had had enough of this bland, throwaway material. And so had Steve Binder, the man hired by NBC to produce and direct the special. Binder knew rock 'n' roll music; he had directed a 1964 rock movie that featured Chuck Berry, the Rolling Stones, and the Supremes. More to the point, he was a longtime Elvis fan. He remembered Elvis when he was raw, rebellious, tough, dangerous—and *that* was the Elvis he wanted for this television special, not some slick, phony, tuxedo-wearing pop star.

To convince Elvis, Binder encouraged him to stroll

down Sunset Boulevard, a popular Hollywood hangout for young people. Remembering the hysteria that greeted his appearance in the 1950s, Elvis was reluctant to go. But he did—and *nobody recognized him!* Even when he tried to draw attention to himself, people walked past as though he didn't exist.

Elvis Presley had literally fallen from sight. Understanding the need to jump-start his career, he placed himself in Binder's hands.

During preparations for the show, Binder and the Colonel clashed constantly. Parker was always mispronouncing the young man's name, calling him "Bindle." He challenged and second-guessed every decision Binder made. Elvis would agree with Parker to his face, but when the Colonel left the room he gave Binder free rein. For his part, Binder felt the Colonel was a phony. "He is the wizard in *The Wizard of Oz*," Binder said, "the guy behind the big black velour with lots of gadgets and neon signs lighting up . . . and he's putting on the whole world."

Elvis was facing television cameras and a live audience for the first time in seven years. As critic Greil Marcus said, "He was putting everything on the line, risking his comforts and his ease for the chance to start over."

If he was nervous, he didn't show it. He emerged dressed in tight, black leather from head to toe, like a hoodlum. The long sideburns, trimmed for the movies, were back. In a way, the television special marked a return to his roots. He was joined by his original band mates Scotty Moore on guitar and D. J. Fontana on drums. But this was no nostalgia trip. Even the old familiar numbers—"Jailhouse Rock," "Love Me Tender," "Lawdy Miss Clawdy"—sounded rougher and more dangerous. Almost a dozen years old, the songs seemed brand-new.

Some of the songs were taped in front of a live, mostly female studio audience. Sitting casually on a bare stage, the crowd buzzing, Elvis joked with the band and told stories about the early days. (He also poked fun at the Beatles, his chief competition.) Other songs featured more polished production numbers. Besides the old material, he introduced new tunes like "Trouble," "Tiger Man," and "Tryin' to Get to You." In a nod to the holiday season, he sang a Christmas tune—not a traditional carol but the soulful "Blue Christmas." Another song, "Let Yourself Go," sung to a crowd of howling, gyrating women, was so sexy that the NBC censor cut it from the show. Just as in the old days, Elvis was getting people all shook up.

The show closed with a new song, "If I Can Dream," written by the program's choral director, Earl Brown. The Colonel had wanted the program to end with "Silent Night." To humor him, Binder taped Elvis singing the song, then threw it away. "If I Can Dream" went on to become one of Elvis's anthems, a powerful number that reflected his spiritual side.

Elvis's performance in the comeback special was everything his movie appearances were not—heartfelt, passionate, raw, steamy, sexy. ("Play it dirty! Play it dirty!" one of his friends shouted during his rendition of "Blue Christmas.") For the first time in years he actually looked like he was having a good time.

The program aired on December 3, 1968, as "Singer Presents Elvis" (although it's known today as "Elvis— The '68 Comeback Special"). It was a big success, the highest-rated program for the week. The soundtrack album, simply titled Elvis—TV Special, reached number eight on the pop charts, his first top-ten album in three years. The single "If I Can Dream" hit number twelve.

Critics loved it. Here, they proclaimed, was the old Elvis brought back to life. "It was the finest music of his life," wrote Greil Marcus. "If ever there was music that bleeds, this was it. Nothing came easy that night, and he gave everything he had—more than anyone knew was there."

In "The '68 Comeback Special," Elvis energized his fading image in front of television cameras and a live studio audience.

Jon Landau, a critic who went on to become Bruce Springsteen's manager, had this to say about the comeback special:

There is something special about watching a man who has lost himself find his way back home. He sang with the kind of power people no longer associate with rock 'n' roll singers. He moved his body with a lack of pre-

tension and effort that must have made [Doors singer] Jim Morrison green with envy. And while most of the songs were ten or twelve years old, he performed them as freshly as though they were written yesterday.

Elvis was back.

* * * * *

The energy and passion of *Elvis—TV Special* spilled over into his next albums.

In early 1969, he returned to the recording studio. Rather than travel to the big RCA studio in Nashville (which many critics felt was too tightly structured for him to do his best work), he chose a Memphis studio called American Sound Studio—a small, casual, relaxed operation that must have reminded him of Sun Records. The young house musicians had grown up listening to Elvis; they understood his early music but were also familiar with the more contemporary sounds. The producer, Chips Moman, had worked with a variety of artists. He was the right person to help Elvis craft a new sound and to take his music to a new level.

Elvis spent eleven days at American Sound Studio, recording thirty-six tracks that ranged from country to soul to pop. Many of these songs recaptured the fire of his earliest work. He recorded his first number-one single in seven years, "Suspicious Minds," a powerful, hard-driving composition. He also taped two top-ten hits—"Don't Cry Daddy" and "In the Ghetto"—and a host of other great tunes, including "Kentucky Rain" and "Any Day Now."

In the studio, Elvis again defied the Colonel. He chose songs by young, independent writers who were not part of the Hill and Range stable. This meant, of course, that Elvis and his manager received no publishing royalties. His decision was vindicated when the album *From Elvis in Memphis* reached number thirteen on the charts.

His next record, *From Memphis to Vegas/From Vegas to Memphis*, also featured material from these sessions.

In 1968 and 1969, Elvis returned to Hollywood just long enough to fulfill his contract. In his final pictures, he tried to break out of the formula. In *Charro!*, a gritty western in the Clint Eastwood mold, he plays a former outlaw standing up to his old gang. "A different kind of role . . . a different kind of man," the advertisements read. For the first and only time Elvis wore facial hair. Till then, in his Elvis Movies, he had even gone without his trademark long sideburns. He was unglamorous and almost unrecognizable behind a scraggly beard.

For *Change of Habit*, his final feature film, he took on the unlikely role of a doctor. In this musical melodrama that featured four songs, Elvis as Dr. John Carpenter fights disease in the inner city and falls in love with a nun played by popular television star Mary Tyler Moore.

Neither movie was very good, but for the first time in seven years Elvis was trying something new, something serious. And then, after *Change of Habit*, he left acting forever. After exhausting the medium of film, and using the medium of television to engineer his comeback, he returned to the place where he first electrified the country in the 1950s—the stage. For the rest of his career, he devoted himself to music.

* * * *

To start Elvis's first road trip in a decade, the Colonel signed a deal with the International Hotel in Las Vegas. It was a surprising choice. Elvis's one previous trip to Vegas, in 1956, had been a disaster. The older audiences didn't appreciate the brash young performer billed as "The Atomic Powered Singer." One critic compared his appearance to "a jug of corn liquor at a champagne party."

This time, however, the Colonel was ready for Vegas. He made sure that Elvis's opening night was the show business event of the year. He took out advertisements all over town, flew in reporters from New York, and invited dozens of celebrities (including Elvis's *Viva Las Vegas* costar, Ann-Margret). Elvis also invited the Memphis legend who had helped him invent his rock 'n' roll sound, Sam Phillips.

Elvis opened at the International Hotel's brand-new showroom on July 26, 1969. From the first notes of his opening number, "Baby I Don't Care," the crowd of two thousand people went wild. Before he reached the chorus they were on their feet, screaming, whistling, clapping, and stomping their feet. Some even stood on their chairs. They kept hollering through "Blue Suede Shoes," "Hound Dog," "What'd I Say," and his final encore, "Can't Help Falling in Love."

The old hysteria was back. Grown women were moved to toss their underwear on the stage. (The International started stocking extra pairs in the bathroom.) From *Variety* to *Newsweek* to *Rolling Stone*, the critics— some who were in grade school when Elvis started his career—were ecstatic. Once again Elvis was King, packing the biggest theater in Vegas twice a night for four weeks. The Colonel negotiated a five-year contract. In exchange for $1 million, Elvis would perform at the International (later named the Hilton) two months every year. It would be the beginning of a long association with the city of Las Vegas.

The Vegas Elvis was a far cry from the Elvis of old. No longer was he backed up by a rough three-piece combo. In 1969, he was joined onstage by three guitarists, a bass player, a keyboard player, a drummer, a twenty-five-piece orchestra, a gospel quartet called the Imperials, and a female backup trio called the Sweet Inspirations—four dozen musicians in all. This new arrangement gave him a fuller, more mature sound.

After his triumphant Vegas gig, he wasted no time

celebrating. Elvis loaded his musicians into a convoy of vehicles and hit the road.

If Elvis had doubts about his return to live performing, they were gone by the end of his first post-Vegas engagement. In Houston, he sold out the 44,500-seat Astrodome for a solid week. After every show he was mobbed, his limousine surrounded by howling, grasping fans, just as in old times.

After Houston, Elvis embarked on a grueling touring schedule. For the next several years he went on a three-week tour almost every month, with a show every night and two shows on Saturdays and Sundays.

If the schedule was rough, the performances themselves were downright exhausting—for performer and audience both. A typical Elvis concert started with a bang. To the sounds of a classical composition called "Also Sprach Zarathustra" (better known as the theme from the movie *2001: A Space Odyssey*), he would bound into the spotlight. Flapping his cape, snapping the microphone cord, he would prowl the stage, charging from one dramatic pose to the next. The pelvis-shaking gyrations of the 1950s were replaced with more-calculated routines, as he worked his favorite karate moves into the act. Sometimes he would stop moving and stand completely still, like a figure in a wax museum, soaking up the screams and the applause.

The audience was an essential part of the Elvis experience. During a concert, he would use dozens of scarves to wipe the sweat from his brow, then toss the scarves into the crowd. In return, women would throw roses, underwear, and their hotel keys onto the stage. Elvis kissed and hugged select audience members. He held their hands while he sang his love ballads. He kept them swooning, hooting, and hollering until he charged off the stage and the announcer boomed, "Ladies and gentlemen, Elvis has left the building."

The live performances of this period were captured in two documentary films, *Elvis, That's the Way It Is* (1970) and *Elvis on Tour* (1972). One reviewer noted that Elvis was probably the only performer with enough fans to make a documentary film a success.

As he entered the 1970s, Elvis also trotted out a whole new look. *Flamboyant* is the word to describe this new image. He dressed in jumpsuits of red, blue, white, or gold, covered with studs, rivets, rhinestones, and semiprecious jewels to match the gold and diamonds on his fingers. The jumpsuits were slit down the front to show off his chest; they ended at the floor in two gigantic bell-bottoms. He often topped off this ensemble with a floor-length Superman cape and a belt buckle the size of a dinner plate. All told, these costumes, which grew more elaborate every year, weighed up to 30 pounds (14 kg)!

The cape called to mind a superhero (like Elvis's boyhood favorite, Captain Marvel). More than anything, the stage outfits of the 1970s were like clothes for royalty. Sparkly, rich, opulent, they were fit for a king—for *the* King.

When he played New York's Madison Square Garden in 1972, Elvis wore a gold-lined cape and a huge belt that said, "WORLD CHAMPION ENTERTAINER." Fans and critics agreed with this description. It was his first concert in New York, and it was a triumph. He broke attendance records and earned critical raves for his four-night stand. Only two weeks after the gig, RCA released an album called *Elvis as Recorded at Madison Square Garden*.

The next year brought his greatest onstage achievement. In January 1973 he returned to television with "Elvis: Aloha from Hawaii," a live concert special that was beamed by satellite to countries in the Far East, including Japan, Thailand, South Vietnam, New

In the 1970s, Elvis Presley traded in black
leather for studded jumpsuits and gaudy jewelry.

Zealand, and Australia. (There were even reports that viewers in Communist China picked up the broadcast.) Later a taped version played in Europe. The Colonel proudly announced that 1.5 billion people—one third of the world's population—saw this single performance. (Many later disputed this figure, however.) In Japan alone, the show broke all records, capturing an unbelievable 98 percent of the audience.

Elvis got so carried away during the show that he tossed a bejeweled cape worth several thousand dollars into the audience, never to be seen again. He could afford it, though—he earned a million dollars from that single performance.

After years of doing what his management team told him to do, Elvis had finally broken free. The concerts of the 1970s now included more of his personal interests, like country and gospel. The songs he sang often mirrored his personal life. "How Great Thou Art" showed his religious side. "American Trilogy" (a medley that included "Dixie" and "The Battle Hymn of the Republic") displayed his patriotism and his love of the South. "Always on My Mind" reflected troubles in his marriage. And "My Way" (already Frank Sinatra's signature song) was a response to all the criticism he had endured in his career.

The years from 1969 to 1973 were incredibly creative ones for Elvis. He ditched the bland, boring movie star image and returned to live performing. He developed a new sound that returned him to the top of the charts. His television appearances (especially "Aloha from Hawaii") brought him to the attention of the whole world. Before his 1968 comeback, he was the King of Rock 'n' Roll. Now, he was known as simply *the King*.

CHAPTER TEN

—— THE ——
DECLINE
AND
FALL

*"An image is one thing, a human
being is another. It's very hard
to live up to an image."*
—Elvis Presley

In the 1970s, Elvis was a road warrior. Between 1969 and
1977 he performed 1,126 concerts, not including the
eight weeks he spent in Las Vegas each year. Most of
those shows were one-night stands. Elvis and his
entourage would pull into a different city every day, set
up the show, perform, get a few fitful hours of sleep at a
hotel, and pack up for the next town. After several years,
these grueling days and nights started taking a physical
and emotional toll on Elvis.

Being on the road meant being away from Graceland
and his family. He saw little of Priscilla and Lisa Marie
during this time. Early in 1972, Priscilla left Elvis and
started dating his karate instructor. The following
August, Elvis sued for divorce in a California court. His
lawyers explained his actions in a statement: "Elvis has

been spending six months a year on the road, which put a tremendous strain on the marriage." In her 1985 autobiography, *Elvis and Me*, Priscilla explained that the marriage failed because she and Elvis never got to be alone.

The split, which became official in October 1973, was friendly. Elvis and Priscilla walked out of the courtroom holding hands. In later years they were both involved in raising Lisa Marie. (Priscilla went on to become a successful actress, starring in several television series and *Naked Gun* movies.)

Elvis said of Priscilla, "She was one of the few girls who was interested in me for me alone." Some think he never recovered from her leaving him.

He also suffered greatly from the death of his mother, even a decade after her passing. When Gladys died, Elvis lost his greatest booster, his protector, and his moral compass. According to Priscilla:

> *It was Gladys who kept Elvis aware of the difference between right and wrong, of the evils of temptation, and of the danger of life in the fast lane. Since Gladys's death, there were no boundaries for Elvis.*

Without boundaries, he started a downward spiral from which he would never recover.

* * * *

> "When you're a celebrity, people treat you nicer. The bad part is, they also tell you what they think you want to hear, which ain't always the truth."
> —Elvis Presley

From the moment he hit the scene in 1956, Elvis never lived a normal life. Famous people rarely do. But Elvis became so famous, so fast, so young, that his view of the world must have been incredibly distorted.

When that first tidal wave of fan adoration struck him, he had to surround himself, as a matter of survival, with a wall of bodyguards. Rather than hire a bunch of strangers, he recruited cousins (like Gene Smith) and high school friends (like Red West, George Klein, and Marty Lacker). Through the years he added other family members and Army buddies to the collection. This group became known as the Memphis Mafia.

For the rest of his adult life, Elvis was almost never without at least a few members of the Memphis Mafia. They joined him in Germany during his Army stint. They lived with him in Hollywood and on various movie locations. They followed him as he toured the country. Back in Memphis, they spent most of their waking hours hanging out at Graceland. Some even lived in Graceland, or in an apartment out back.

Their job was to keep Elvis entertained. He had a childish streak, and the money to indulge it. He loved practical jokes. In Hollywood, he bought a pet chimpanzee named Scatter that he would dress up in a suit and parade around town in a limousine. He and the Memphis Mafia were kicked out of the ritzy Beverly Wilshire Hotel after a water-pistol fight got out of hand. Back at Graceland, the gang loved to play with Elvis's expensive toys, including motorcycles and three-wheeled scooters.

After his return from the Army, Elvis started to withdraw from the outside world. In earlier days he liked to mingle with fans, stop at the Graceland gates to chat and sign autographs. But eventually he couldn't go out without being mobbed, knocked down, trampled, even stripped of his clothes. It became dangerous as well as an annoyance.

Over the years Elvis became more and more secluded. He started living like a recluse. The Memphis Mafia helped to shelter him. They ran all his errands, followed all his orders, and laughed at all his jokes. When he toured, they protected him as he moved from a private plane to a private limo to the stage to a hotel suite and back to the plane. He was completely cut off from the concerns of everyday life. When he did see people, it was in a huge arena, where they were screaming and swooning and adoring him by the thousands.

His girlfriend, Linda Thompson, called it "a nice abnormal life." Abnormal it certainly was. They lived like nocturnal animals, sleeping during the day and recording (and partying) at night. Once, when Elvis was in the hospital, he covered the windows with aluminum foil to keep out the daylight and made the staff reverse their sleep schedules.

By the mid-1970s Elvis had created his own little world, where night was day and his word was law. He lived at the center of this universe, but many others shared the space. When he toured, his entourage consisted of dozens of musicians and crew members, his girlfriend, his father, stepbrothers, cousins, the Colonel, the Memphis Mafia, a doctor, a karate teacher, a hairdresser—and a jewelry salesman on twenty-four-hour alert, just in case Elvis wanted to buy diamonds at three in the morning.

* * * *

"Sharing money is what gives it its value."

—Elvis Presley

With his power, fame, and wealth, Elvis was able to indulge himself in many ways. When it came to shopping, he was a chronic overspender. Born poor, he grew up dreaming of money. When he had money beyond his wildest dreams, he could not control his spending. Whatever Elvis wanted, Elvis bought.

Cars were his weakness. He could never seem to resist an expensive automobile. Any expensive car would do—a Rolls Royce, a Mercedes, a Messerschmidt—but he was especially partial to Cadillacs. According to legend, he arrived for his 1956 screen test in two Cadillacs, one for him and one for his guitar. In 1960 he bought a Cadillac limousine, had it coated with twenty-four-carat-gold paint, and installed a television, a record player, and an electric shoe-shine machine in it. (That Cadillac, worth an estimated $100,000, is today on display at the Country Music Hall of Fame in Nashville.) He once bought fourteen Cadillacs in a single day, at a dealership just down the street from Sun Records. During the last ten years of his life, he owned at least one hundred expensive vehicles, most of them Caddies.

He couldn't resist jewelry, either. Onstage and off, his body was encrusted with flashy baubles—gold chains, bracelets, medallions, gold- and silver-plated belt buckles, and rings on every finger. He even designed some of his own jewelry. One of his favorite rings featured an 11.5-carat diamond and the letters TCB, which stood for Takin' Care of Business, his personal motto.

His most expensive hobby was collecting airplanes. He bought several, which he used on tour. He named one of the planes *Lisa Marie*, after his daughter. In 1976 he flew from Memphis to Denver—a $16,000 trip—just to pick up some of his favorite peanut-butter sandwiches. It was probably the most expensive snack in history.

As much as he spent on himself, Elvis gave away as much—or more. His generosity was legendary. He gave away more than a hundred cars (mostly Cadillacs) to friends, bodyguards, nurses, and maids—a million dollars' worth of cars, by one estimate. He gave away an equal amount of jewelry, including TCB rings for the Memphis Mafia. If somebody admired his clothing, he literally gave them the shirt off his back. He bought his nurse a mink coat, his maid a house. He gave singer Sammy Davis, Jr., a $30,000 black sapphire ring, explaining, "Nobody thinks of giving a rich man anything."

His generosity was not limited to friends and family. Every Christmas he gave large sums to Memphis charities (as much as $100,000 every year). He would hand $500 to a blind pencil seller on the street, or buy a motorized wheelchair for a woman he read about in the newspaper. He bought a yacht and donated it to actor Danny Thomas for his St. Jude Children's Research Hospital.

Once when he was shopping for Cadillacs after midnight (the dealers *always* stayed open late when they saw Elvis coming), he saw a young couple peering through the window of the dealership. He invited them inside, told them to pick their favorite, and wrote a check. Later, a Colorado newscaster reporting on Elvis's generosity joked, "Mr. Presley, I would not like to have a Cadillac— I'd rather have a little sports car." The next day he received a Cadillac Seville (the littlest and sportiest car Cadillac made), compliments of Mr. Presley.

After a while, his generosity turned into an obsession; he seemed desperate to have people like him. His spending got wildly out of control. The more he spent, the more he had to tour. The more he toured, the more pressure he felt. And the more pressure he felt, the more he turned to self-destructive habits.

Elvis Presley's life was filled with contradictions. Maybe the ultimate contradiction had to do with his image. At the beginning of his career, he was an innocent, God-fearing kid who acted the rebel onstage—and was blamed for corrupting the youth of America.

In later years, however, he totally reversed the situation. Whereas on the stage and screen he portrayed a wholesome, clean-cut, all-American boy, his life away from the fans was getting wilder and more self-destructive.

Drugs were Elvis's downfall. He was first introduced to them in the Army, when he took dexadrine (an amphetamine, or "upper") to stay awake during guard duty. According to members of the Memphis Mafia, he returned to amphetamines in Hollywood to keep his weight down and to give him energy for early-morning shoots. When those pills gave him trouble sleeping, he was prescribed sleeping pills.

As his career started to go flat in the 1960s, he became, according to Priscilla, "lonely and depressed." He was prescribed antidepressant drugs. Then, during the grueling tours of the 1970s, he started developing genuine health troubles—back pain, digestive problems, and glaucoma (ailments that landed him in the hospital several times between 1973 and 1977). For these illnesses his doctor gave him painkillers and other drugs.

Interestingly, Elvis never drank and rarely smoked. Further, he preached about the evils of illegal drugs. He justified his own drug use by saying he took only drugs prescribed by a doctor. In 1970 he even took a trip to Washington, D.C., to volunteer his services for President Richard Nixon's fight against drugs and receive a Bureau of Narcotics and Dangerous Drugs badge from the president himself.

Under the influence of drugs, Elvis's behavior became more and more erratic in the 1970s. He took late-night trips to the Memphis morgue to look at the dead bodies. He started to believe that he had spiritual powers to heal the sick.

He became very nervous, even paranoid. The behavior was in part justified. During the 1970s he received kidnapping and death threats. After one such threat in Las Vegas he performed a show carrying one gun in his

In 1970, Elvis Presley traveled to the White House to offer his services in President Richard Nixon's campaign against drugs.

belt and one in his boot. At another Vegas show, four drunks rushed the stage; Elvis knocked one of them into the audience and received a seven-minute standing ovation. He started wearing a bulletproof vest in public. The Memphis Mafia kept him even more isolated. If fans strayed too close, they were sometimes roughed up by the King's bodyguards.

Elvis loved guns and other kinds of weapons. His collection included .44 Magnums, a gold-handled Python, a turquoise-handled Colt .45, rifles, and semiautomatics. He often carried a Derringer pistol in his boot. According to his bodyguards, he even traveled with an M-16 rifle and a Thompson submachine gun.

He never shot at animals (he hated hunting) or people. Television sets, however, were fair game. In a famous story, he was said to have blasted a hole in a Graceland television when a singer he didn't like, Robert Goulet, appeared on the screen. (According to Priscilla, he inherited a wicked temper from his parents.) On another occasion, he and the boys filled a swimming pool with flashbulbs and shot them with BB guns. Cleaning the pool took two days.

Elvis's eating habits also contributed to his decline. He liked to consume large quantities of rich, fried, fatty foods like bacon, eggs, and cheeseburgers. His favorite snack was fried peanut-butter-and-banana sandwiches washed down with Pepsi. A good southern boy, he also loved grits and biscuits and gravy. Although he ate this way his whole life, he exercised less when he got older and gained a good deal of weight. By some accounts, he tipped the scales at 250 pounds (113 kg), up from his earlier trim 185 pounds (84 kg). The weight gain, and efforts to lose that weight in a hurry, probably aggravated his poor health.

His unhealthy lifestyle started destroying his musical career. The momentum he had gained from "The '68 Comeback Special" screeched to a halt. Some years in the 1970s he never even entered a recording studio. On a few occasions he recorded, halfheartedly, in the Graceland living room. In order to crank out three albums every year, RCA recorded his live performances or repackaged songs from earlier albums.

Onstage, his drug use left him in a fog. His speech was often slurred. He occasionally forgot the words to songs. Some nights he clutched the microphone stand just to keep from falling over.

As his performances faltered, the press started to turn

on him. After a 1977 Detroit concert, a local critic wrote, "It is damning Presley with faint praise to say that he stunk the joint out. If he appeared live and in concert tonight in my backyard, I wouldn't bother to raise the window shade. . . . Presley is old, fat, and virtually immobile. At best, he is a parody of himself."

＊＊*

Although he was one of the most famous people in the world, Presley was a mystery to many of his fans. For most of his career, the Colonel and the Memphis Mafia kept details of his private life hidden. That all changed, however, in the fall of 1977.

On August 1, a New York publisher released a book called *Elvis: What Happened?*, which contained interviews with three former members of the Memphis Mafia—Red West, Sonny West, and Dave Hebler—who had all been fired the year before. In this tell-all tale, the disgruntled ex-bodyguards revealed, according to the cover, "THE DARK OTHER SIDE OF THE BRIGHTEST STAR IN THE WORLD!" They reported drug abuse and violent behavior. Although fans refused to believe the book, the media picked up on some of the more sensational stories.

The book cracked the wall of privacy around Elvis. For the first time, there was confusion in the King's court. Still, no one was prepared for what would happen two weeks later.

CHAPTER ELEVEN

—— THE ——
KING is DEAD

*"Elvis would not want anyone to
think that he had no flaws or
faults. But now that he's gone,
I find it more helpful to remember his good qualities, and I
hope you do, too."*
— Rev. C. W. Bradley at Elvis
Presley's funeral

On June 26, 1977, Elvis Presley performed at Market
Square Arena in Indianapolis. Like any other Elvis concert, the show ended with the customary announcement:
"Ladies and gentlemen, Elvis has left the building." He
flew to Memphis in the *Lisa Marie* and went to Graceland to rest up for his next tour.

Fast-forward to early morning, August 16. At 4 or 5
A.M., Elvis played racquetball on his private court. He
went to bed at his usual time and awoke later that same
morning to go to the bathroom, bringing with him a
book, *The Scientific Search for the Face of Jesus.* His girlfriend, Ginger Alden, warned him not to fall asleep.
"Okay, I won't," Elvis replied. Those were his final words.

That afternoon at about two-thirty, Alden found him
on the bathroom floor, face down on the red shag carpet.

According to the police report, his body was "slumped over in front of the commode . . . his arms and legs were stiff, and there was discoloration in his face." Members of the Memphis Mafia called for an ambulance, which took him to Baptist Memorial Hospital.

Doctors tried to revive him, but it was too late. Elvis Aron Presley was pronounced dead at 3:30 P.M. on August 16, 1977. He was forty-two years old.

The cause of death was listed as "cardiac arrhythmia," an irregular heartbeat. "He had the arteries of an eighty-year-old man," a hospital employee reported. "His body was just worn out."

In the years that followed, rumors of Elvis's drug abuse continued to circulate. In 1979, the ABC television program "20/20" reported that his death resulted from "polypharmacy," the deadly mixing of several drugs taken at the same time. An autopsy indicated the presence of as many as ten different drugs. It was later revealed that Elvis's doctor, George Nichopoulos, had prescribed to Elvis 5,684 narcotic and amphetamine pills between January 20 and August 16, 1977—an average of twenty-five pills a day. On August 15 alone, the day before he died, Elvis had filled eight different prescriptions.

In 1979, Dr. Nichopoulos was charged by the Tennessee Board of Medical Examiners with "indiscriminately prescribing 5,300 pills and vials for Elvis in the seven months before his death." In 1980 he lost his license for three months. He was later found not guilty on charges of "willingly and feloniously" overprescribing drugs for Elvis.

The funeral of Elvis Presley was one of the most amazing events the country has ever seen. It was the old Presley hysteria one last time. It revealed the depth of affection and adoration that Americans felt for the King of Rock 'n' Roll.

Less than an hour after the death was announced, people started lining up at the gates of Graceland. By noon the next day, the crowd was estimated at twenty thousand.

Fans from around the world, including the Soviet Union, sent flowers to the mansion at 3764 Elvis Presley Boulevard. FTD, the national floral network, reported its biggest day in history, selling 2,155 arrangements. By the afternoon of August 17, every bud and blossom in Memphis had been sold; reinforcements were called in from California and Colorado (5 tons in all). Flowers arrived at Graceland in the shape of hound dogs, guitars, crowns, crosses, and Bibles.

Elvis's father, Vernon Presley, decided to make his son's body available for a public viewing. At 3 P.M. on August 17, the Graceland gates swung open. Fans marched silently up the long driveway. Just inside the front door of Graceland, Elvis's body—dressed in a white suit, a light-blue shirt, and a white tie—lay in an open copper coffin. The mourners walked slowly across white sheets that covered the foyer's red carpeting. At the casket they sobbed, gasped, wailed. Many prayed aloud. Some collapsed, overcome with grief.

Outside Graceland, thousands more fans crushed against the gates, struggling hysterically to get inside. Dozens fainted as the intense Memphis heat and humidity took their toll. A team of paramedics was stationed near the gates. Police helicopters hovered overhead. Vendors passed through the crowd selling T-shirts and souvenirs. As reporter Bob Greene wrote, "It was a scene of hysteria that matched the wildest Presley concert."

By the time the Graceland gates closed, at 5:30 P.M., twenty thousand fans had passed through. They had traveled from all over the United States and the world. They were, wrote Pete Hamill in the *New York Daily News*, "almost all working people; people who drove trucks and worked in gas stations and spent their youth in roadside

After Elvis Presley's death in 1977, hundreds
of thousands of fans mobbed the
Graceland gates in Memphis.

taverns, listening to tales of their heartbreak hotel."
Many abandoned their jobs or spent their life savings to
be there to see their dead idol. Tragically, two young
women died themselves when a drunk driver crashed into
the crowd outside Graceland.

Reporters by the hundreds also arrived from around
the world. All three television networks aired special doc-
umentaries about Elvis. When CBS chose *not* to lead off

its evening news with a story about his death, millions of viewers changed channels, giving CBS its lowest ratings in years. Radio stations broadcast a constant stream of Elvis's hits. The *National Enquirer* paid $5,000 for a snapshot of Elvis in his coffin. With the gruesome picture on the cover, the issue sold 6.7 million copies, the newspaper's all-time record.

His death made banner headlines around the world. In Cologne, Germany, the headline read, "*Elvis Presley tot! Erstickt!*" ("Elvis Presley dead! Struck down!"). In Thailand, the *Bangkok Post* reported that "people from all walks of life in Bangkok expressed shock yesterday over the sudden death of Elvis Presley." In South Africa, a Johannesburg newspaper wrote, "Black, white, young, and old mourned Elvis the Pelvis, the truck driver who became a legend."

On August 18, the Presley family held a private memorial service in the music room at Graceland. Colonel Tom Parker, Ann-Margret, guitarist Chet Atkins, and Priscilla Beaulieu Presley were among the 150 invited guests. Some of Elvis's favorite gospel singers sang his favorite hymns, including "How Great Thou Art," a song that Elvis had recorded and included in most of his concerts. Most Memphis radio stations observed two minutes of silence as the funeral got under way.

Then a caravan of seventeen white Cadillac limousines, led by a silver Cadillac and the white Cadillac hearse with Elvis's body, made its way along the 4-mile (6-km) route to the cemetery. Another brief ceremony followed at the mausoleum, surrounded by all those floral arrangements. (It took a hundred vans to transport the flowers from Graceland to the cemetery.)

Elvis Aron Presley was buried at the Forest Hill Cemetery in Memphis. After vandals tried (unsuccessfully) to steal his casket from the mausoleum, his body and the body of his mother, Gladys Love Presley, were moved to the Meditation Garden at Graceland. There, under a statue of Jesus on the cross, they were reburied next to a plaque honoring Elvis's stillborn twin brother, Jesse Garon Presley. They were later joined by father and husband Vernon Elvis Presley, who died in 1979 at the age of sixty-three.

The day after Elvis's funeral, an estimated fifty thousand fans visited his tomb at the cemetery. At the family's request, nearly every fan took home a single flower from the thousands of arrangements that blanketed the lawn.

CHAPTER TWELVE

── LONG ──
LIVE THE KING

"A whole industry was built around an animated mouse named Mickey. The next could be Elvis Presley."
—Joseph Rascoff, former business manager of the Presley estate

The story of Elvis Presley does not end at his grave site. If anything, it becomes even more interesting after August 16, 1977, the day of his untimely death.

In the weeks after Elvis's funeral, the world took a renewed interest in his career. Radio stations started playing his songs again. Stores sold out Elvis records in a matter of days. To meet the demand, RCA kept its plant in Indianapolis—which could press 250,000 albums a day—running day and night. Later, the company ended up subcontracting pressing plants around the globe. By October 1977, several Elvis records were back on the charts. In the first year after his death, he sold an astonishing two hundred million records. (Before his death he had sold five hundred million, more than any other pop star.)

Colonel Tom Parker was also working overtime in

the days after Elvis's death. By the time of the funeral, he had already struck a deal giving a company called Factors, Inc., the exclusive rights to market Elvis products. (He had Vernon Presley sign the contract on the day of his son's funeral.) "Nothing has changed," the Colonel allegedly said on the day of Elvis's death. "This won't change anything."

Marketing Elvis, of course, was nothing new. As early as 1956, the Colonel was peddling his client's name on charm bracelets, dog tags, and blue suede shoes. But this was nothing compared to the rush of Elvis products after his death. By 1979, a shopping mall had risen across the street from Graceland, filled with stores devoted to nothing but Elvis. Here a devoted fan could buy Elvis pins, pillows, pennants, postcards, Christmas tree ornaments, guitar-shaped hairbrushes, watches, knives, belt buckles, and trash cans—over seventy Elvis items in all.

Characteristically, the Colonel pocketed half the money coming in from Elvis merchandise—indeed, he was earning more from Elvis's name than the Presley family. In 1980, Priscilla Presley and the other executors of Elvis's estate asked a court to look into the Colonel's deal with Factors, Inc. The court charged Parker with "enriching himself by mismanaging Presley's career."

In 1983, Elvis's estate tried to sue the Colonel. He responded that he could not be sued in a U.S. court because he was not a U.S. citizen, a fact he had never revealed until that moment. The case was settled out of court.

During his forty-two-year life and his twenty-three-year career, Elvis Presley was an artistic and financial sensation. After his death, he became a phenomenon. His popularity has not diminished; if anything, it has increased. Elvis lives on as an industry, a myth, a cult hero.

There have been many popular, successful singers in history. What sets Elvis apart is his special relationship with his audiences. As the title of one of his posthumous (after-death) albums puts it: *50,000,000 Elvis Fans Can't Be Wrong.*

This unprecedented relationship between fan and star goes back to the earliest days of Elvis Presley's career. He was always concerned about his fans, and he worked hard to give them what they wanted. Before it became too dangerous, he enjoyed mingling with them, signing autographs, and posing for photos. During his later concerts he tried to make contact with audience members by touching them, kissing them, or tossing them his sweat-soaked scarves.

In the eyes of his fans, Elvis was worth admiring not just for his talent but because he was a good person. (Many fans chose to ignore the allegations of drug abuse and bizarre behavior.) He loved his mama, he worshiped God, and he was always generous to friends and strangers alike. Above all, he never forgot his humble roots. He never left Memphis. He never lost his southern accent or his love of southern food. He was one of them—with, perhaps, a little more talent, fame, and money. "I guess you could say Elvis was what we'd like to be," said one fan. "He's one of us—and yet he's our ideal."

When Elvis died, his heartsick fans felt a true sense of loss. But in some ways, as the Colonel said, nothing would change. The fans continue to preserve his memory with Elvis memorabilia, Elvis conventions, and Elvis fan clubs.

Today there are nearly five hundred Elvis fan clubs on the planet. The largest, in Leicester, England, has twenty-two thousand members; the smallest, in the Philippines, has only seven. These groups function as families, social clubs, and charity organizations. A Vermont club president worked for years in a successful effort to get an Elvis postage stamp. Oklahoma fans are devoting their lives to having Elvis become a posthumous Medal of Freedom recipient. In Pittsburgh, the largest American fan club (with eleven hundred members) endowed an Elvis Aron Presley Visiting Fellowship at a hospital and maintained an International Elvis Fund to help fans in Eastern Europe "keep in touch with the Elvis world."

Fans around the world also gather at Elvis conventions, which sometimes draw as many as ten thousand people. Here they can buy souvenirs, listen to speeches by people who knew Elvis, and of course talk and swap stories about their idol.

For many fans, the highlight of the year is the annual Tribute Week held in Memphis on the anniversary of Elvis's death. Every August, Graceland is the center of the Elvis nation. If you're a fan, you figure out a way to get there. As writer Stanley Booth said in 1982, "The anniversary of his death promises to become a holiday like Christmas or the Fourth of July."

The nine-day observance features dozens of events, including tours of Sun Records, Humes High School, and Elvis's karate studio; a Graceland-sponsored luncheon for fan club presidents; a concert; a laser show; and a 5-kilometer (3-mile) run. A local hotel sponsors a contest in which fans decorate their windows with an Elvis theme.

The highlight of Tribute Week is the candlelight vigil held on August 15, the eve of the anniversary of his death. Thousands of fans, including hundreds from fan clubs in England, Sweden, Japan, and other countries, start lining up that morning so they can be the first through the Graceland gates. At midnight, those gates swing open and fans, each carrying a lighted candle, proceed silently up the driveway to the Presley family grave site.

One fan compared Tribute Week to "Elvis boot camp." "If you can survive one week in the heat and humidity," she said, "staying up until four every morning, eating bad food—then you know you're a true fan."

The battle for the "truest" fan is one that's closely fought. For some fans, their love for Elvis has turned into an obsession. They think nothing of spending next month's rent on an Elvis video, an Elvis china toothpick holder, or Elvis wallpaper. They have seen all his movies, bought every book and compact disc. They have "ELVIS" license plates on their cars. They have memorized the most trivial Elvis facts: his Army ID number (53310761), the name of his private pilot (Milo High), his favorite hamburger joint (The Gridiron).

Some of the more devoted fans turn their homes into shrines; their Elvis objects swallow up their houses and yards. In California, a fan spent a million dollars building a house that's an exact replica of Graceland. A Virginia woman has a miniature Graceland in her yard, complete with a mini-Elvis and an "audience" of thirty Barbie dolls.

The center of the Elvis universe is located at 3764 Elvis Presley Boulevard (formerly U.S. Highway 51) in Memphis: Graceland. In 1982, his ex-wife, Priscilla, decided to open Graceland to the public all year round. Today, tours of the home cover most of the first floor and the basement. The second floor, including the room where he died, is closed to the public.

The interior of Graceland is often described as flamboyant or tacky, and it is. When Elvis redecorated much of the house in the 1970s, that style was common. Colors range from royal blue to gold. (The grand piano, a gift from Priscilla, is covered with gold leaf.) Mirrors hang everywhere. A deep shag carpet sometimes covers the ceiling, as it does in Elvis's favorite room, the Jungle Room. According to legend, he saw a television commercial for a Memphis furniture store, drove down, picked out all the Jungle Room furniture in thirty minutes, and had it delivered that same day. The room has a

Polynesian theme: fake-fur-upholstered couches whose arms are gargoyles, lamps carved to resemble tikis (images of Polynesian gods), and an illuminated waterfall. It's a wild sight.

Everything in the house was bought new. Antiques reminded Elvis of his poor upbringing. "When I was growing up in Tupelo," he said, "I lived with enough antiques to do me for a lifetime."

A tour of Graceland is a complete entertainment experience, like an Elvis theme park. Across the street, fans can view his bus and private plane, the *Lisa Marie*, tour a collection of his automobiles, shop for souvenirs at the Elvis mall, and see a short movie about his life. Behind the mansion, a trophy room exhibits Elvis mementos, from his seventh-grade report card to his 126 gold and platinum records. Also on display are his letters from President Nixon and Federal Bureau of Investigation chief J. Edgar Hoover, as well as jumpsuits, jewelry, guns, paintings, and gifts he received from fans.

For many, the high point of the Graceland tour is the Meditation Garden, where Elvis and the Presley family are buried. Elvis's grave is marked by an eternal flame and a bronze plaque. On his tomb, fans often leave behind love letters, floral displays (shaped like hound dogs, guitars, and teddy bears), and their tears.

Over the years, Graceland has become a major tourist attraction. The number of visitors has increased every year since 1982. In 1994 the mansion hosted more than seven hundred thousand fans. It is one of the most visited homes in America, second only to the White House.

Graceland is owned and operated by Elvis Presley Enterprises, Inc., a division of Presley's estate. The house and all his assets will be turned over to his daughter, Lisa Marie Presley, on her thirtieth birthday in 1998. Lisa Marie has two children. In 1994 she married pop star Michael Jackson, who like Elvis has sold millions of

**Lisa Marie Presley and singer Michael Jackson
after their 1994 marriage**

records and been criticized for his sensual performing
style. Less than a year later they announced they were fil-
ing for a divorce.

*****

*"We are trying hard to actually
give birth to him again."*
—Joseph Rascoff, former business
manager of the Presley estate

Elvis Presley was not just a musician and an actor. To the
people who promoted him, he was a product—a very

profitable product that made lots of money for RCA, the Colonel, movie studios, and many others, as well as for himself. Today, people are still cashing in on Elvis. His motto—"Takin' Care of Business"—has never been more appropriate.

Indeed, Elvis is worth *more* dead than alive. According to a 1984 estimate, he made ten times more money during the seven years after his death than he earned in twenty-three years of actual performing. In 1988 he made the cover of *Forbes*, a business magazine, as the highest-paid *dead* entertainer of the year. *Forbes* figured that if the Presley estate were put on the market, the rights to marketing his name could probably fetch $100 million or more.

In 1984, a Tennessee judge ruled that those valuable rights to Elvis's name and likeness belong to his estate. In other words, if somebody wants to sell a memento with his picture on it, they have to get the estate's permission and give it a percentage of the profits.

Today Elvis Presley Enterprises, Inc., earns millions by licensing his image on everything from ceramic masks to lampshades to shampoo. It fields ideas from would-be makers of Elvis knickknacks every day and claims to turn down products that are "tacky, pornographic, or associated with 'Elvis is alive' rumors." And it searches out companies that are using the Elvis name or image illegally and threatens them with lawsuits if they don't stop.

The public's appetite for Elvis objects keeps increasing. Elvis fans can buy everything from liquor decanters to board games, from beach towels to Love Me Tender Moisturizing Milk Bath. Over the years, some stranger items have slipped through the cracks—and have been criticized for being too crassly commercial. These include a wine called Always Elvis (advertised as "The wine Elvis would have drunk, if he drank wine"); a dog food, Love Me Tender Chunks, for pelvic pooches; and greeting cards containing fake vials of Elvis's sweat.

Dead or alive, Elvis still sells records too. Go into a record store today and you'll be able to buy more of his albums than those of any other artist in the history of recording. After his death, RCA continued to release as many as three albums a year. Some were repackaged sets of songs that had already been released. Others featured live performances or unreleased tunes. In 1983, an RCA employee discovered a treasure trove of unreleased tapes at Graceland. Two years later, on the fiftieth anniversary of Elvis's birth, RCA released much of this material in a six-record set.

Bookshelves groan under the weight of hundreds of books about Elvis. The authors include his uncle, step-brothers, nurse, secretary, karate teacher, real estate agent, ex-wife, and ex-wife's ex-boyfriend. Nearly all the members of the Memphis Mafia have cashed in with books. They also speak to fan clubs or sell videotapes in which they discuss their relationship with Elvis.

Many of Elvis's friends have made money selling items he once owned or gave them as gifts. These objects go for a king's ransom. At a 1994 auction in Las Vegas, his 1969 Mercedes-Benz limousine sold for $321,500. A rhinestone jumpsuit fetched $68,500. Even a simple pair of sunglasses went for $26,450. People will pay anything, it seems, to have a piece of the King.

In the whole wide Elvis world, perhaps the strangest citizens are the Elvis impersonators—the men (and sometimes women) who would be King.

Elvis impersonators make a living by imitating Presley in concert. They imitate his singing, his gyrations, his appearance. (Most choose to mimic the 1970s Vegas Elvis, rather than the 1950s rebel Elvis. Almost no one picks the 1960s movie Elvis.) Some fans boycott the impersonators, whom they consider disrespectful. To others, however, seeing an impersonator is a fun way to relive the excitement of a live Elvis performance.

By some estimates, the world contains more than two thousand Elvis impersonators, in all shapes, sizes, and colors. These Elvis wanna-bes spend thousands of dollars on exact replicas of Elvis's rhinestone jumpsuits. Some train with vocal coaches to mimic his voice, or study karate to get his moves down pat. One impersonator had plastic surgery to make his face more closely resemble Elvis's. Another had his name legally changed to Elvis Presley. A couple of impersonators claim to be Elvis's illegitimate sons; they both tried to take the name Elvis Aron Presley, Jr., and one was sued by Elvis's estate. There are even two different sets of skydiving Elvis impersonators, one of which appeared in the movie *Honeymoon in Vegas*.

Recently, a group called the Elvis Presley Impersonators International Association (EPIIA) held a convention at a hotel in suburban Chicago. Ron Bessette, the EPIIA president, said he founded the organization "to provide some ethics and standards, to overcome the old stigma that the guys are just goofing around." Nearly a hundred Elvis impersonators gathered to promote their craft. They included three part-time impersonators who work by day as a jockey, a mayor, and an anesthesiologist; impersonators named Ted Presley (no relation) and Dr. Nazar Sayegh; and black impersonators, women impersonators, Mexican impersonators (El Vez, who sang "You Ain't Nothin' But a Chihuahua"), and seven-year-old impersonators. Many performers brought their own fan clubs, with as many as five hundred members, mostly female.

The convention featured classes open to the public, including "How to Become an Elvis Impersonator," in which Dave Carlson analyzed a fellow performer:

A team of skydiving Elvis impersonators, known as the Flying Elvi, poses for a publicity shot before taking to the skies.

First of all, this guy was shaking his right *leg. Elvis always shook his* left *leg, held the mike in his left hand, and curled his lip to the left side.*

Of course, the convention included live shows by all the impersonators. While they performed, their female fans screamed and scrambled for sweat-soaked scarves.

* * *
*

Many observers note that the adoration of Elvis has taken on elements of a religious cult. "This has the makings of the rise of a new religion," said a Mississippi minister in a *Time* magazine article. "Elvis is the God, and Graceland the shrine. There are no writings, but that could be his music." And some of the fans, he added, "even say he is rising again."

In perhaps the strangest twist of all, a few devoted (some might say demented) fans believe that Elvis has been resurrected, or that he never died at all.

The rumors started in 1988, after the publication of a book that claimed to include an interview with Elvis called *Is Elvis Alive?* The rumors were fueled by bizarre stories in tabloid newspapers like the *National Examiner* ("ELVIS IS PERFORMING MIRACLES IN A LEPER COLONY") or the *Sun*, which claimed that Russian astronauts photographed a statue of Elvis on Mars. Soon, Elvis was being spotted at a Minnesota car race, a Texas department store, a Michigan Burger King. The president of an Elvis fan club in California reported that he calls her periodically. A record promoter from Texas claimed he has been called by Elvis "hundreds of times" and plans to release an album recently recorded by Elvis and a book cowritten by Elvis.

These believers back up their claims with questionable logic. They point out that his middle name is spelled differently on his tombstone ("Aaron") than it is on his birth certificate ("Aron"). They also note that the numbers in Elvis's date of death (8/16/1977) add up to 2001, which is the name of a movie (*2001: A Space Odyssey*) whose theme song was the King's theme song in later years. Furthermore, Elvis once rented Suite 2001 in a building at 2001 Union Avenue. Others say that if you rearrange the letters, *Elvis* spells *lives*. These facts, they argue, prove without a doubt that Elvis is still alive.

In a book called *Elvis After Life*, Dr. Raymond A.

Moody, Jr., shares stories of people who claim to have had psychic experiences involving Elvis. According to one woman, all her Elvis records mysteriously melted the night he died. A police officer says he found his missing son using information supplied by Elvis in a dream.

If Elvis is dead, as most sensible people agree, there's one way fans can keep his memory alive. A California scientist is selling copies of Elvis's genes, copied from a strand of his hair. The microscopic pieces of Presley DNA will be used to make earrings and necklaces. From now on, true believers can show their love by having a piece of their idol hanging around their neck.

*　*　*　*

Love him or hate him, you have to agree: Elvis is a one-of-a-kind artist. In life and in death, he has redefined the concept of fame. Can you think of any other performer who has thousands of people imitating him for a living? Can you name one other dead celebrity who, year after year, has seven hundred thousand people traveling miles and miles just to place a flower on his grave?

During the forty-two years, seven months, and eight days he spent on the planet, Elvis Aron Presley kicked off a revolution in music and popular culture. The reverberations of that revolution are still being felt today.

Thanks to compact discs and videotapes, his legacy will be preserved for generations to come. This American original will keep fascinating, captivating, confounding, and shocking listeners well into the future.

Long live the King.

──── ELVIS: ────
THE MUSIC

Behind all the myths, the legends, and the tall tales, there is the music. Elvis recorded dozens of albums during his lifetime. He put out thirty-three movie soundtracks alone, in addition to live albums and greatest-hits collections. After his death in 1977, Elvis's songs were endlessly repackaged in multivolume series like *Elvis's Gold Records* and *Elvis: A Legendary Performer.* The following is a listening guide to some of Elvis's best recordings:

• *The Top Ten Hits* (RCA 6383-R). An excellent overview of his entire musical career, this two-record collection of thirty-eight top-ten songs takes the listener from "Heartbreak Hotel" (1956) and "Hound Dog" (1956) to "The Wonder of You" (1970) and "Burning Love" (1972).

• *The Complete Sun Sessions* (RCA 6414-1-R). Where it all began. This disc includes all the singles Elvis recorded with Sam Phillips for Sun Records between 1953 and 1955. It also features some songs that were never released and some experimental takes. You can even hear snippets of Presley and Phillips discussing their craft. Songs include "Blue Moon of Kentucky," "Good Rockin' Tonight," and "Mystery Train."

• *From Elvis in Memphis* (RCA LSP 4155). This 1969 album shows Elvis at the peak of his post-Hollywood comeback. Songs include "In the Ghetto," "Any Day Now," and "Long Black Limousine."

• *From Memphis to Vegas/From Vegas to Memphis* (RCA 6020). The first of these two discs picks up where *From Elvis in Memphis* leaves off; it includes "Suspicious Minds," a 1969 song that was Elvis's first number-one hit in seven years. The second disc is a live album, recorded at the International Hotel in Las Vegas.

• *His Hand in Mine* (RCA LPM 2328). Elvis grew up listening to religious music, and in this album he pays tribute to his gospel roots. Songs include "I'm Gonna Walk Dem Golden Stairs" and "Swing Low, Sweet Chariot."

• *Reconsider, Baby* (RCA AFL1-5418). This collection displays Elvis at his bluesiest. Among the blues classics included are "I Feel So Bad," "Down in the Alley," and "Merry Christmas Baby."

ELVIS:
THE MOVIES

During a fourteen-year span, Elvis made thirty-one feature films. Some (*Jailhouse Rock* and *Viva Las Vegas*) were interesting and energetic. Others (*Kissin' Cousins* and *Girl Happy*) were embarrassingly mediocre. However, every movie Elvis ever made—good, bad, or indifferent—is available today on video, a tribute to his staying power.

Love Me Tender (1956)
Loving You (1957)
Jailhouse Rock (1957)
King Creole (1958)
G.I. Blues (1960)
Flaming Star (1960)
Wild in the Country (1961)
Blue Hawaii (1961)
Follow That Dream (1962)
Kid Galahad (1962)
Girls! Girls! Girls! (1962)
It Happened at the World's Fair (1963)
Fun in Acapulco (1963)
Kissin' Cousins (1964)
Viva Las Vegas (1964)
Roustabout (1964)
Girl Happy (1965)
Tickle Me (1965)

Harum Scarum (1965)
Frankie and Johnny (1966)
Paradise, Hawaiian Style (1966)
Spinout (1966)
Easy Come, Easy Go (1967)
Double Trouble (1967)
Clambake (1967)
Stay Away, Joe (1968)
Speedway (1968)
Live a Little, Love a Little (1968)
Charro! (1969)
The Trouble With Girls (and How to Get Into It) (1969)
Change of Habit (1969)

Documentary Films

Elvis: That's the Way It Is (1970)
Elvis on Tour (1972)

— SELECTED —
BIBLIOGRAPHY

Few figures in entertainment history have been analyzed, discussed, and debated as much as Elvis Presley. Countless words have been written by journalists, music critics, historians, family members, friends—even Elvis's cook and his karate teacher.

Today, two decades after his death, Elvis still shows up regularly in newspapers and magazines. In researching this book I have referred to articles from the *New York Times*, the *Chicago Tribune*, the *Chicago Sun-Times*, the *Los Angeles Times*, the *San Diego Union-Tribune*, *GQ*, *Smithsonian*, *Life*, and the *Atlantic Monthly*.

In discussing events after his death, I have also relied on my own reporting for publications such as *Campus Voice*, *Special Report*, and the *Boston Globe*.

The following books served as primary sources. I am greatly indebted to their authors.

Doll, Susan. *Elvis: A Tribute to His Life*. Lincolnwood, Ill.: Publications International, 1989.

Greene, Bob. *American Beat*. New York: Atheneum, 1983.

Gregory, Neal, and Janice Gregory. *When Elvis Died*. Mahwah, N.J.: Pharos Books, 1992.

Guralnick, Peter. *Last Train to Memphis: The Rise of Elvis Presley*. Boston: Little, Brown, 1994.

Hopkins, Jerry. *Elvis: The Final Years.* New York: St. Martin's, 1981.

Marcus, Greil. *Dead Elvis.* New York: Doubleday, 1991.

———. *Mystery Train.* New York: Dutton, 1975.

Pearlman, Jill. *Elvis for Beginners.* New York: Writers and Readers Publishing Cooperative, 1986.

Presley, Priscilla Beaulieu, with Sandra Harmon. *Elvis and Me.* New York: Putnam, 1985.

Quain, Kevin, ed. *The Elvis Reader.* New York: St. Martin's, 1992.

Stern, Jane, and Michael Stern. *Elvis World.* New York: Viking, 1987.

Worth, Fred L., and Steve D. Tamerius. *Elvis: His Life from A to Z.* Chicago: Contemporary Books, 1990.

INDEX

143